AQA STUDY G

GCSE 9–1
ANIMAL
FARM

BY GEORGE ORWELL

SCHOLASTICIC

Author Annie Filmer-Bennett

Reviewer Rob Pollard

Editorial team Rachel Morgan, Audrey Stokes, Lesley Densham, Kate Pedlar

Typesetting Jayne Rawlings/Oxford Raw Design

Cover design Dipa Mistry and Jason Cox

App development Hannah Barnett, Phil Crothers and RAIOSOFT International Pvt Ltd

Illustration Rosalia Ra.Ro Radosti

Photographs
page 4: The use of cover image from ANIMAL FARM written by George Orwell, published by Penguin Modern Classics, 2000. First published by Martin Secker & Warburg Ltd, 1945. Published in Penguin Books, 1951. This edition first published by Martin Secker & Warburg Ltd in the Complete Works of George Orwell series, 1987. Published in Penguin Books with an Introduction and a new Note on the Text, 1989. Reprinted in Penguin Classics, 2000. Copyright 1945 by Eric Blair. This edition copyright © the Estate of the late Sonia Brownell Orwell, 1987. Introduction copyright © Malcolm Bradbury, 1989. Note on the Text copyright © Peter Davison, 1989. Reproduced by permission of Penguin Books Ltd; page 13: butcher's knife, Laralova/Shutterstock; page 15: clover, Christine Glade/Shutterstock; page 17: horse, David Katrencik/Shutterstock; page 23: apples in barrel, Ljupco Smokovski/Shutterstock; page 34: nails and string, Scorsby/Shutterstock; page 38: broken egg, Ljupco Smokovski/Shutterstock; pages 39 and 42: blood splatters, Yeti studio/Shutterstock; page 42: £5 note, RUBEN M RAMOS/Shutterstock; page 45: whisky barrel, Alexlukin/Shutterstock; page 46: green ribbon, onair/Shutterstock; page 49: boar and piglets, Mny-Jhee/Shutterstock; page 71: Stalin, US Army Signal Corps/Wikimedia Commons; page 72: Trotsky, Wikimedia Commons; Hitler, German Federal Archives/Wikimedia Commons; page 74: manacles, Moussa81/istock; chains, valeo5/Shutterstock; page 78: pocket watch, Neirfy/Shutterstock; page 81: beer, givaga/Shutterstock; milk churn, lantapix/Shutterstock; page 82: Animal Farm 1st edition, Wikimedia Commons; page 90: girl sitting exam, Monkey Business Images/Shutterstock; page 93: notepad and pen, TRINACRIA PHOTO/Shutterstock

Designed using Adobe InDesign

Published in the UK by Scholastic Education, 2020
Book End, Range Road, Witney, Oxfordshire, OX29 0YD
A division of Scholastic Limited
London – New York – Toronto – Sydney – Auckland
Mexico City – New Delhi – Hong Kong
SCHOLASTIC and associated logos are trademarks and/or registered trademarks of Scholastic Inc.
www.scholastic.co.uk
© 2020 Scholastic Limited
1 2 3 4 5 6 7 8 9   0 1 2 3 4 5 6 7 8 9

British Library Cataloguing-in-Publication Data
A catalogue record for this book is available from the British Library.

ISBN 978-1407-18343-5
Printed and bound by Bell and Bain Ltd, Glasgow
Papers used by Scholastic Limited are made from wood grown in sustainable forests.

Note from the publisher:
Please use this product in conjunction with the official specification and sample assessment materials. Ask your teacher if you are unsure where to find them.

Contents

Check your answers on the free revision app or at www.scholastic.co.uk/gcse

How to use this book

This Study Guide is designed to help you prepare effectively for your AQA GCSE English literature exam question on *Animal Farm* (Paper 2, Section A).

The content has been organised in a sequence that builds confidence, and which will deepen your knowledge and understanding of the novel step by step. Therefore, it is best to work through this book in the order that it is presented.

HOW TO REVISE!

This Study Guide uses the Penguin Modern Classics edition.

Know the plot

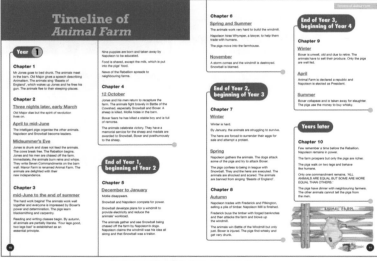

1 It is very important that you know the plot well: to be clear about what happens and in what order. The **timeline** on pages 10–11 provides a useful overview of the plot, highlighting key events.

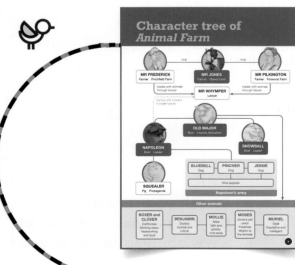

The **character tree** on page 9 introduces you to the main characters of the text.

The chronological section

2 The **chronological section** on pages 12–53 takes you through the novel, chapter by chapter, providing plot summaries and pointing out important details. It is also designed to help you think about the structure of the novel.

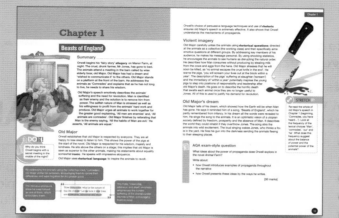

This section provides an in-depth exploration of themes or character development, drawing your attention to how Orwell's language choices reveal the novel's meaning.

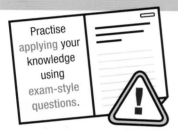

Practise applying your knowledge using exam-style questions.

The novel as a whole

3 The second half of the guide is retrospective: it helps you to look back over the whole novel through a number of relevant 'lenses': characters, themes, Orwell's language, forms and structural features.

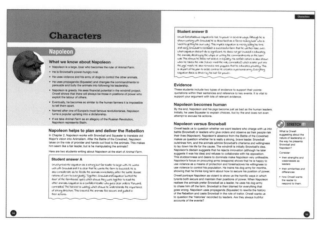

Doing well in your AQA Exam

Stick to the **TIME LIMITS** you will need to in the exam.

4 Finally, you will find an extended 'Doing well in your AQA exam' section which guides you through the process of understanding questions, and planning and writing answers.

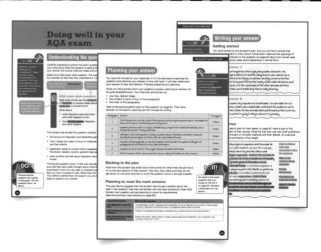

Features of this guide

The best way to retain information is to take an active approach to revision.

Throughout this book, you will find lots of features that will make your revision an active, successful process.

 SNAPIT!

Use the Snap it! feature in the revision app to take pictures of key concepts and information. Great for revision on the go!

DEFINEIT!

Explains the meaning of difficult words from the set texts.

Callouts Additional explanations of important points.

Words shown in **purple bold** can be found in the glossary on page 94.

Regular exercise helps stimulate the brain and will help you relax.

Find methods of relaxation that work for you throughout the revision period.

DOIT!

Activities to embed your knowledge and understanding and prepare you for the exams.

NAILIT!

Succinct and vital tips on how to do well in your exam.

STRETCHIT!

Provides content that stretches you further.

REVIEW IT!

Helps you to consolidate and understand what you have learned before moving on.

Revise in pairs or small groups and deliver presentations on topics to each other.

FOR HIGH-MARK QUESTIONS, SPEND TIME **PLANNING** YOUR ANSWER!

AQA exam-style question

AQA exam-style sample questions based on the extract shown are given on some pages. Use the sample mark scheme on page 86 to help you assess your responses. This will also help you to understand what you could do to improve your response.

FREE REVISION APP

- The **free revision app** can be downloaded to your mobile phone (iOS and Android), making **on-the-go revision** easy.

- Use the revision calendar to help map out your revision in the lead-up to the exam.

- Complete multiple-choice questions and create your own **SNAP**IT! revision cards.

  www.scholastic.co.uk/gcse

Online answers and additional resources

All of the tasks in this book are designed to get you thinking and to consolidate your understanding through thought and application. Therefore, it is important to write your own answers before checking. Some questions include tables where you need to fill in your answer in the book. Other questions require you to use a separate piece of paper so that you can draft your response and work out the best way of answering.

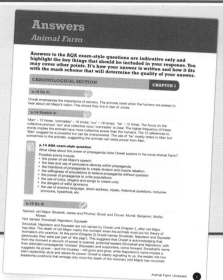

Get plenty of sleep, especially the night before an exam.

LOOK AFTER YOURSELF

Help your brain by looking after your whole body!

Once you have worked through a section, you can check your answers to Do it!, Stretch it!, Review it! and the exam practice sections on the app or at **www.scholastic.co.uk/gcse**.

An introduction to your AQA modern text

NAILIT!

- Keep a close watch on the time in your exam. Don't spend more than 45 minutes on the *Animal Farm* question or you will have less time to write your answers to the poetry anthology question in Section B and the unseen poetry questions in Section C.

- Take special care over spelling, punctuation and grammar as there are four extra marks available for these.

Why study *Animal Farm*?

Although *Animal Farm* was written more than 70 years ago, it has kept its appeal and still has a strong immediate relevance. Orwell published his novel in 1945 to explore ideas about power, corruption and propaganda. He exposes the ways that truth and lies infuse political systems and how populations are controlled. Although Orwell references the events of the Russian Revolution, he is not attacking communism, but rather the abuse of power under *any* banner. These are important issues to consider today as 'fake news' and power-hungry leaders dominate our world. Orwell exposes the harmful consequences of brutal leadership. He also emphasises the importance of education as a means of combatting indoctrination. The farm becomes a microcosm of a totalitarian state, which is ironic. Orwell wants us to question the truths distributed by those in power, and their motives.

In *Animal Farm*, the animals on Manor Farm decide to overthrow the farmer, Mr Jones, who is a cruel leader. They believe they can run the farm for the benefit of all animals. The Revolution itself is surprisingly easy to achieve; however, sticking to the principle of Animalism (communism) proves to be more of a challenge.

Animal Farm in your AQA exam

Animal Farm is examined in Section A (the first part) of the second AQA GCSE English Literature exam, Paper 2 Modern texts and poetry. Here is how it fits into the overall assessment framework:

Paper 1 Time: **1 hour 45 minutes**	Paper 2 Time: **2 hours 15 minutes**
Section A: Shakespeare	**Section A: Modern prose or drama: *Animal Farm***
Section B: 19th-century novel	Section B: Poetry anthology
	Section C: Unseen poetry

There will be **two** questions on *Animal Farm*. You must answer **one** of them. You should spend **45 minutes** planning and writing your answer to the question. There are 30 marks available for the *Animal Farm* question, plus four extra marks for good **vocabulary, spelling, sentences and punctuation** (VSSP, sometimes called 'SPaG').

A character tree

The 'character tree' on page 9 should help you to fix in your mind the names of the characters and their relationships.

Timeline of *Animal Farm*

The timeline on pages 10–11 provides a visual overview of the plot, highlighting key events which take place over the course of the novel. It will also help you to think about the structure of the novel.

Character tree of *Animal Farm*

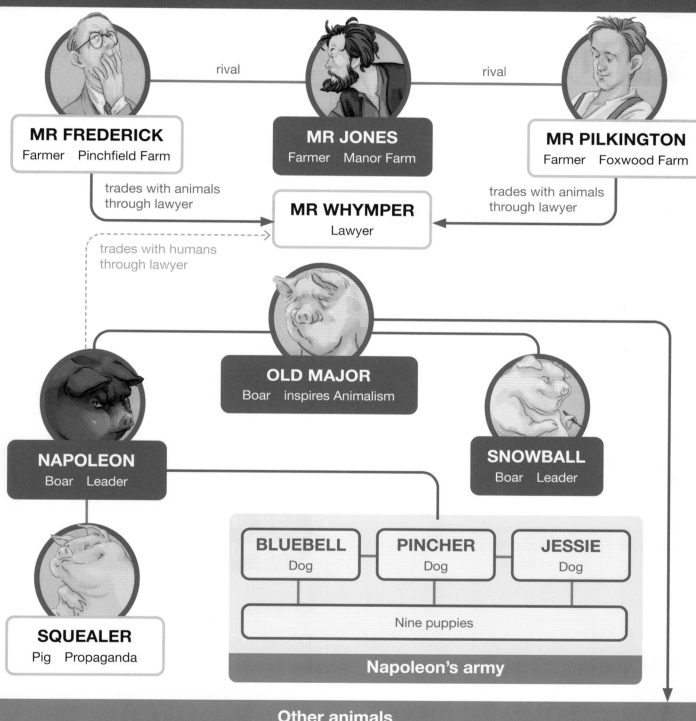

MR FREDERICK
Farmer   Pinchfield Farm

MR JONES
Farmer   Manor Farm

MR PILKINGTON
Farmer   Foxwood Farm

rival

rival

trades with animals through lawyer

trades with animals through lawyer

MR WHYMPER
Lawyer

trades with humans through lawyer

OLD MAJOR
Boar   inspires Animalism

NAPOLEON
Boar   Leader

SNOWBALL
Boar   Leader

SQUEALER
Pig   Propaganda

BLUEBELL
Dog

PINCHER
Dog

JESSIE
Dog

Nine puppies

Napoleon's army

Other animals

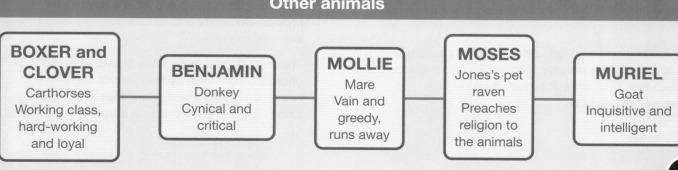

BOXER and CLOVER
Carthorses
Working class, hard-working and loyal

BENJAMIN
Donkey
Cynical and critical

MOLLIE
Mare
Vain and greedy, runs away

MOSES
Jones's pet raven
Preaches religion to the animals

MURIEL
Goat
Inquisitive and intelligent

Timeline of *Animal Farm*

Year 1

Chapter 1

Mr Jones goes to bed drunk. The animals meet in the barn. Old Major gives a speech describing Animalism. The animals sing 'Beasts of England', which wakes up Jones and he fires his gun. The animals flee to their sleeping-places.

Chapter 2

Three nights later, early March

Old Major dies but the spirit of revolution lives on.

April to mid-June

The intelligent pigs organise the other animals. Napoleon and Snowball become leaders.

Midsummer's Eve

Jones is drunk and does not feed the animals. The cows break free. The Rebellion begins. Jones and his men are chased off the farm. Immediately, the animals burn reins and whips. They write Seven Commandments on the barn wall. Manor Farm is renamed Animal Farm. The animals are delighted with their new independence.

Chapter 3

mid-June to the end of summer

The hard work begins! The animals work well together and everyone is impressed by Boxer's power and determination. The pigs learn blacksmithing and carpentry.

Reading and writing classes begin. By autumn, all animals are partially literate. 'Four legs good, two legs bad' is established as an essential principle.

Nine puppies are born and taken away by Napoleon to be educated.

Food is shared, except the milk, which is put into the pigs' food.

News of the Rebellion spreads to neighbouring farms.

Chapter 4

12 October

Jones and his men return to recapture the farm. The animals fight bravely in Battle of the Cowshed, especially Snowball and Boxer. A sheep is killed. Mollie hides in the barn.

Boxer fears he has killed a stable boy and is full of remorse.

The animals celebrate victory. They have a memorial service for the sheep and medals are awarded to Snowball, Boxer and posthumously to the sheep.

End of Year 1, beginning of Year 2

Chapter 5

December to January

Mollie disappears.

Snowball and Napoleon compete for power.

Snowball develops plans for a windmill to provide electricity and reduce the animals' workload.

The animals gather and see Snowball being chased off the farm by Napoleon's dogs. Napoleon claims the windmill was his idea all along and that Snowball was a traitor.

Chapter 6

Spring and Summer

The animals work very hard to build the windmill.

Napoleon hires Whymper, a lawyer, to help them trade with humans.

The pigs move into the farmhouse.

November

A storm comes and the windmill is destroyed. Snowball is blamed.

End of Year 2, beginning of Year 3

Chapter 7

Winter

Winter is hard.

By January, the animals are struggling to survive.

The hens are forced to surrender their eggs for sale and attempt a protest.

Spring

Napoleon gathers the animals. The dogs attack some of the pigs and try to attack Boxer.

The pigs confess to being in league with Snowball. They and the hens are executed. The animals are shocked and scared. The animals are banned from singing 'Beasts of England'.

Chapter 8

Autumn

Napoleon trades with Frederick and Pilkington, selling a pile of timber. Napoleon Mill is finished.

Frederick buys the timber with forged banknotes and then attacks the farm and blows up the windmill.

The animals win Battle of the Windmill but only just. Boxer is injured. The pigs find whisky and get very drunk.

End of Year 3, beginning of Year 4

Chapter 9

Winter

Boxer is unwell, old and due to retire. The animals have to sell their produce. Only the pigs are well fed.

April

Animal Farm is declared a republic and Napoleon is elected as President.

Summer

Boxer collapses and is taken away for slaughter. The pigs use the money to buy whisky.

Years later

Chapter 10

Few remember a time before the Rebellion. Napoleon remains in power.

The farm prospers but only the pigs are richer.

The pigs walk on two legs and behave like humans.

Only one commandment remains, 'ALL ANIMALS ARE EQUAL BUT SOME ARE MORE EQUAL THAN OTHERS.'

The pigs have dinner with neighbouring farmers. The other animals cannot tell the pigs from the men.

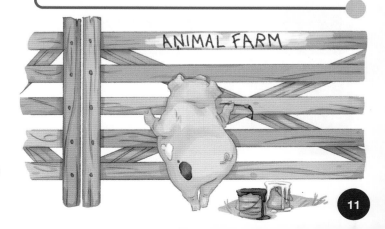

Beasts of England

Summary

Orwell begins his 'fairy story' **allegory** on Manor Farm, at night. The cruel, drunk farmer, Mr Jones, has gone to bed. The animals attend a meeting in the barn called by wise elderly boar, old Major. Old Major has had a dream and 'wished to communicate it' to the others. Old Major stands on a platform at the front of the barn. He addresses the animals as 'Comrades' and explains that as he has not long to live, he needs to share his wisdom.

Old Major's speech emotively describes the animals' suffering and the need for revolution. Man is identified as their enemy and the solution is to remove him from power. The selfish nature of Man is stressed as well as his willingness to profit from the animals' hard work and produce. Old Major urges all animals to work together for the greater good explaining, 'All men are enemies' and, 'All animals are comrades'. Old Major finishes by reiterating that Man is the enemy saying, 'All the habits of Man are evil.' He asserts, 'All animals are equal.'

Old Major

Orwell establishes that old Major is respected by everyone. They are all happy to lose sleep to listen to him. This shows the power of the pigs at the start of the novel. Old Major is respected for his wisdom, majesty and kindness. He sits above the others on a stage; this implies that old Major is seen as superior to the other animals, making his statements about equality somewhat **ironic**. He speaks with impressive eloquence.

Old Major uses **rhetorical language** to inspire the animals to revolt.

DO IT!

Why do you think Orwell begins with a secret meeting in the middle of the night?

By addressing the animals using the collective noun, 'comrades', old Major unites his audience, encouraging them to ignore their differences and work together for the greater good.

The inclusive pronouns show he sees himself as one of them, which emboldens them.

"
'Now, comrades, what is the nature of this life of ours? Let us face it: our lives are miserable, laborious and short.'
"

The triple, 'miserable, laborious and short' emotively emphasises the current suffering of the animals under the rule of Man, encouraging them to rebel.

Orwell's choice of persuasive language techniques and use of **rhetoric** ensures old Major's speech is extremely effective. It also shows that Orwell understands the mechanisms of propaganda.

Violent imagery

Old Major carefully unites the animals using **rhetorical questions** directed at the animals as a collective (the working class) and then specifically aims emotive questions at different groups. By addressing key members of his audience, he makes his message personal. By using shocking statistics, he encourages the animals to see humans as disrupting the natural order. He describes how Man consumes without producing by stealing milk from the cows and eggs from the hens. Old Major stresses that he will soon be killed, as 'no animal escapes the cruel knife in the end'. He warns the pigs, 'you will scream your lives out at the block within a year'. The description of the pigs' suffering at slaughter ('scream') and the immediacy of 'within a year' potentially inspires the young pigs to step into positions of responsibility and leadership after old Major's death. He goes on to describe the horrific death that awaits each animal once they are no longer useful to Jones. All of this is used to justify his demand for revolution.

Old Major's dream

Old Major tells of his dream, which showed how the Earth will be when Man has gone. He says it reminded him of a song, 'Beasts of England', which he partly remembered from infancy. In his dream all the words were revealed to him. He sings the song to the animals. It is an optimistic vision of a utopian society defined by freedom, prosperity and the absence of Man. It describes the world they could inhabit if they overthrow Jones. The song stirs the animals into wild excitement. The loud singing wakes Jones, who thinks a fox is in the yard. He fires his gun into the darkness sending the animals fleeing to their sleeping places.

AQA exam-style question

What ideas about the power of propaganda does Orwell explore in the novel *Animal Farm*?

Write about:

- how Orwell introduces examples of propaganda throughout the narrative

- how Orwell presents these ideas by the ways he writes.

[30 marks]

STRETCH IT!

Re-read the whole of old Major's speech in Chapter 1 (beginning, 'Comrades, you have heard…'). Look at the frequency of the lexical choices 'Man', 'comrades', 'our' and 'he'. What does this frequency suggest about the balance of power and the potential power of the animals?

Character and theme essentials

Mr Jones

The cruel, drunk farmer is portrayed as useless. He neglects his animals. There are no positive aspects of Mr Jones; he is established as a two-dimensional figure of authority. He **personifies** abusive leadership.

Old Major

This wise old boar is greatly admired and although he does not live to rule over Animal Farm, he inspires a generation of animals to overthrow the humans. His dream is inspirational but old Major's ideas are idealistic and rely on establishing complete equality. Old Major appears to have been cared for by the humans but he still wants to overthrow them for the good of all animals.

Boxer and Clover

Carthorses Boxer and Clover are introduced together, like a couple. Boxer is immensely strong, powerful and caring. He is respected and admired by the other animals. Clover is maternal, caring and protective of more vulnerable animals. This is shown when she makes a wall around the orphaned ducklings with her foreleg.

NAIL IT!

Your AQA exam asks you to explain Orwell's methods (A02). One key method is his use of characterisation in which he personifies the animals to represent aspects of human society.

Look at how Orwell creates sympathy for key working-class characters, Boxer and Clover, and maintains this throughout.

Mollie

The pretty mare is younger than the carthorses: she is shallow and motivated by sugary treats. She is vain and selfish, showing off her ribbons, and it is clear that she is attention seeking.

Benjamin

This cynical donkey is the oldest animal on the farm: he is grumpy, sullen and pessimistic. He never laughs as 'he saw nothing to laugh at'.

Moses

The human's tame raven is an unusual pet. Ravens are associated with Apollo, the god of prophecy, in Greek mythology. They are also **symbols** of bad luck. Moses was a Christian prophet. Notice how Moses the raven does not participate in the meeting but is nonetheless introduced by Orwell, showing his significance.

Leadership

Old Major's leadership is strong. Although he delivers an emotive and rousing speech and vision of the future, he also warns the animals of the dangers of copying men's vices. Perhaps old Major's vision is overly idealistic. Is it ever possible to achieve complete equality? Orwell wants us to question what makes a great leader. Vision is essential but a pragmatic and logical approach to creating a functioning society is also crucial. By portraying Man as parasitic, old Major unites the animals by giving them a common enemy. This speech mirrors the Communist Manifesto of Karl Marx, which culminates in the words, 'The workers have nothing to lose…but their chains. Workers of the world, unite!' (See page 73.)

Revolution and rebellion/hopes and dreams

Orwell shows how the seeds of revolution can be planted within a population. By portraying their current conditions as horrific, and then describing a utopian vision for a post-revolution future, old Major unites the animals and encourages them to rebel. The song, 'Beasts of England', highlights one way in which leaders spread their messages. The song is both serious and humorous with a simple **rhythm** and **rhyme**. This captures the imaginations of all animals. The 'golden future time' is portrayed as a time that is both precious and within reach: 'Soon or late the day is coming'. The oppressive methods of control – 'bit…spur…whips' – will be removed, and if they work hard, the animals will achieve this blissful state of existence on Earth.

REVIEW IT!

1 Where and when do the animals gather for their meeting?

2 Which characters represent the working class?

3 Who is old Major? Why is he important?

4 Who is the cynical character in the barn?

5 What does Clover do that shows her caring nature?

6 Which animal does not come to the meeting?

7 What words does old Major use to collectively describe the animals?

8 Record five rhetorical questions used in old Major's speech.

9 Complete the quotation, 'Man is the only creature who consumes without _____.'

10 What is old Major's criticism of man removing the cows' milk?

11 What happens with the rats? What does this show about the animals? Why is it ironic?

12 What does Orwell suggest about the revolution by calling it a 'golden future time'?

13 List five symbols of oppression that old Major includes in his song, 'Beasts of England'.

14 How are Boxer and Clover similar? How are they different? Why is this significant?

15 Which human vices does old Major warn against in his speech?

16 What does Orwell suggest about Mr Jones from his opening description?

17 What does Orwell suggest about Mr Jones from his closing description?

18 How does Orwell make the song 'Beasts of England' easy to remember? Why is this important?

19 Who is the most foolish character in this chapter? Why do you think this?

20 To what extent could old Major's dream be said to be simply a fantasy? Write a paragraph explaining your thoughts.

Chapter 2

Animalism

Summary

Three nights later, old Major dies and is buried at the bottom of the orchard. Over the next three months, the animals secretly prepare for rebellion. The intelligent pigs organise and try to educate the other animals. Two young boars, Napoleon and Snowball, become leaders. Their characters are contrasted. Napoleon is huge, fierce-looking and usually gets his own way. However, Snowball is more lively and clever with his words. The other pigs are unimportant except a small, overweight boar named Squealer, an impressive speaker who can be very persuasive when arguing. Napoleon, Snowball and Squealer organise the key elements of old Major's speech into a belief system which they call 'Animalism'. They hold secret meetings in the barn and explain the principles of Animalism to the others. Some animals remain loyal to Jones to begin with and Mollie, the pretty mare, worries about losing luxury items such as sugar and ribbons. However, soon they are all united except for Jones's tame raven, Moses, who is a clever speaker and Jones's spy. He tells the animals of a heavenly place, where animals could go after death, called Sugarcandy Mountain. The pigs argue hard to persuade the animals that Sugarcandy Mountain does not exist. The two carthorses, Boxer and Clover, are keen to adopt Animalism and help to pass on the principles to the other animals.

DEFINE IT!

clover – a green plant that some animals love to eat

linseed cake – a treat given to animals

Sugarcandy Mountain

Moses is created by Orwell to **satirise** the power of the Christian Church. The Biblical Moses rescued the Egyptians from slavery but Moses the raven preaches a message that implies they remain enslaved.

This version of heaven includes infinite rest, endless food, and treats for all. The impossibility of such luxury speaks volumes about the struggles of the working class, whose symbolic desires represent rest, food and reward.

> "…a mysterious country called Sugarcandy Mountain, to which all animals went when they died…somewhere up in the sky… In Sugarcandy Mountain it was Sunday seven days a week, clover was in season all the year round, and lump sugar and linseed cake grew on the hedges. The animals hated Moses because he told tales and did no work, but some of them believed in Sugarcandy Mountain, and the pigs had to argue very hard to persuade them that there was no such place."

This suggests they will have to establish an alternative system of belief to rival that of organised religion.

Rebellion

Summary

One night, at Midsummer, Jones gets drunk and the animals are left unfed. Spontaneously, the Rebellion begins. A cow breaks in the door of the store-shed and all the animals feed from the food bins. Jones and his men appear with whips to get the animals back inside. All the animals attack them and chase them off the farm. Mrs Jones sees what is going on and leaves unnoticed by the animals, followed by Moses. The animals have won! Immediately, they check that no other humans are hiding on the farm. Then they throw the bits, nose-rings, dog-chains and knives down the well and burn reins, halters, blinkers, nosebags and whips. Snowball also burns ribbons, which he considers to being like human clothes. Following Snowball's example, Boxer throws his straw hat on to the fire. Napoleon rewards all the animals with extra food; they sing 'Beasts of England' seven times in a row and sleep soundly.

Re-read Moses' description of Sugarcandy Mountain. Compare and contrast this vision of the afterlife with the reality of Animal Farm before and after the Rebellion. What point do you think Orwell is making?

'Animal Farm'

Summary

The next day, the animals are delighted with their freedom. They rush to the top of the knoll in the pasture where they can see the farm and feel ecstatic to think that it is all theirs. They then do a tour of inspection all around the farm. They are frightened to enter the farmhouse but Snowball and Napoleon lead the way. They are shocked by the luxuries inside. They vote to preserve the farmhouse as a museum. After breakfast, Snowball and Napoleon call a meeting. They inform the other animals that the pigs have taught themselves to read and write. The pigs then rename Manor Farm 'Animal Farm' and reduce the complex principles of Animalism down to 'Seven Commandments' which are painted on the side of the barn.

Snowball then urges the animals to start harvesting the hay. However, the cows make a loud fuss as they need to be milked. The pigs milk the cows. Snowball takes the animals to bring in the harvest leaving Napoleon behind with the milk. When the animals return in the evening, the milk has gone.

THE SEVEN COMMANDMENTS

1. Whatever goes upon two legs is an enemy.
2. Whatever goes upon four legs, or has wings, is a freind.
3. No animal shall wear clothes.
4. No animal shall sleep in a bed.
5. No animal shall drink alcohol.
6. No animal shall kill any other animal.
7. All animals are equal.

The day after the victory, the animals gather at the top of the knoll to look at their land.

Extract 1

> …there was a knoll that commanded a view of most of the farm. The animals rushed to the top of it and gazed round them in the clear morning light. Yes, it was theirs – everything that they could see was theirs! In the ecstasy of that thought they gambolled round and round, they hurled themselves into the air in great leaps of excitement.

The collective ownership shows that they believe they have equal shares in the farm.

However, their ecstatic state suggests this is just as fantastical as Sugarcandy Mountain, which foreshadows the inevitable end of this heaven on earth.

The pastoral scene is idyllic. **Pathetic fallacy** is used to imply good has conquered evil and shows that the revolutionaries have a vivid vision of the future. The new age of Animalism begins with the best of intentions.

Extract 2

Orwell shows the animals' fear of the humans by their reluctance to enter the farmhouse.

> …the farmhouse…was theirs too, but they were frightened to go inside. After a moment, however, Snowball and Napoleon butted the door open…They tiptoed from room to room… gazing with a kind of awe at the unbelievable luxury, at the beds with their feather mattresses, the looking-glasses, the horsehair sofa…Some hams hanging in the kitchen were taken out for burial, and the barrel of beer in the scullery was stove in with a kick from Boxer's hoof, otherwise nothing in the house was touched…All were agreed that no animal must ever live there.

Orwell implies that the animals need guidance and leadership.

Where humans would have consumed the hams, the animals lay them to rest, showing they are caring and kind, treating the victims of human oppression (under the old regime) with a dignity never afforded to them in life.

These items show the extent to which humans used animal products to create luxury goods. The animals have been sacrificed for the benefit of this elite species.

This is significant as the farmhouse represents hierarchy and this decision shows the animals are remaining true to the principles of Animalism set out in old Major's speech.

DEFINE IT!

gambolled – frolicked

knoll – small hill or mound

pastoral – rural

STRETCH IT!

What is foreshadowed about the future of life on Animal Farm in Extract 2?

DO IT!

Explain briefly to what extent you agree with this student's view of the importance of the farmhouse.

> It's clear that the animals are shocked by the luxury in which the humans lived. Orwell portrays the inequality between the men and animals to show there was good reason for the Rebellion and that this level of luxury is extremely unfair. It is made clear that the farmhouse is a place the animals fear and that they are disgusted by the behaviour of the humans. When Mollie tries to take a ribbon, it **symbolises** her desire to restore her old relationship with the humans but, mostly, the animals seem united in their hatred of the farmhouse and what it represents.

AQA exam-style question

What ideas about the consequences of revolution does Orwell explore in the novel *Animal Farm*?

Write about:

- how Orwell introduces the consequences of revolution throughout the narrative

- how Orwell presents these ideas by the ways he writes.

[30 marks]

Character and theme essentials

Napoleon (boar)

Napoleon's power increases rapidly. He relies on his physical bulk to appear impressive, rather than words. Significantly, Napoleon's first words are, 'Never mind the milk, comrades!' By using his enormous bulk to divide the milk from the animals, Orwell shows he will use brute force as a method of control. His use of **imperatives** and commands show he will be an authoritarian ruler. The animals obey Napoleon without question. His repetitive references to them as his 'comrades' becomes increasingly ironic as we can see this type of leader believes he is superior and abuses the trust placed in him by his followers.

Snowball (boar)

Snowball is more intelligent than Napoleon. He personally tackles the more challenging obstacles to Animalism, represented by Mollie's love of ribbons and sugar. Snowball leads the destruction of objects of oppression, 'the nose-rings, the dog-chains, the cruel knives'.

Snowball writes the new name 'ANIMAL FARM' on the gate. This shows his intelligence, and his abilities to write and plan which prove to be strengths later in the novel. He also writes the Seven Commandments on the barn wall and reads them out. In the early stages of the revolution, Snowball seems dedicated to the true spirit of Animalism.

Leadership

Napoleon and Snowball represent different types of leadership.

Together:

- they translate old Major's speech into a working system
- they organise meetings with the animals to teach them
- after the Rebellion, they break down the door to the farmhouse
- in the barn, they introduce the Seven Commandments.

Both Napoleon and Snowball use Squealer (the voice of propaganda) to 'turn black into white'. The name implies he is an informant and provider of information but also someone who will not be silenced.

Orwell wants us to consider whether the two leaders working together will be successful. Is it possible to have equality within a leadership team? Orwell is exposing some of the ways that leaders both inspire their followers and give guidance and orders that they will be encouraged to follow.

Rules and order

The Seven Commandments establish the principles of Animalism. What is Orwell asking us to consider about laws and the ways in which rules are established? Did all the animals agree to these rules? Who makes them? It is interesting to consider that no consequences for disobedience are established at this stage. It is assumed that the animals are united in purpose. Orwell wants us to question those in authority and become active participants in politics.

REVIEW IT!

1　When does old Major die? Where is he buried?

2　What are the names of the three most powerful pigs?

3　What does Mollie not want to give up?

4　What is Sugarcandy Mountain, who preaches about it, and what does it represent?

5　When does the Rebellion take place?

6　What triggers the Rebellion?

7　What does Mrs Jones do?

8　What do the animals burn and fling down the well?

9　Complete the quotation, 'Yes it was theirs – everything they could see was _____.'

10　What is disturbing about the mattresses and sofa?

11　What happens to the hams?

12　Name the Seven Commandments.

13　Who writes the commandments on the barn wall?

14　How are Napoleon and Snowball different? How are they similar?

15　What happens to the cows' milk?

16　What does Orwell suggest about Napoleon from his opening description?

17　What does Orwell suggest about Snowball from his opening description?

18　Why are Napoleon's first words significant?

19　In your opinion, who is the most dangerous character in this chapter? Why?

20　To what extent could Animalism be said to be doomed? Write a paragraph explaining your thoughts.

Chapter 3

The hard work begins!

Summary

The animals work hard to bring in the harvest and it is a great success. The pigs do not do any physical work but direct and supervise the others. It is considered natural that the pigs should assume leadership due to their superior knowledge. With the humans gone, there is more food for all of the animals. There are difficulties when harvesting corn later in the year without a threshing machine, but the pigs' cleverness and Boxer's strength provide a solution. Everyone is impressed by Boxer's power and determination. He gets up earlier than the others to put in extra work. When faced with any problem or setback, his response is always, 'I will work harder!' Mollie on the other hand is lazy, as is the cat, who disappears when there is work to be done but reappears with excellent excuses at mealtimes. Everyone else works according to their capacity apart from Benjamin, the donkey, who seems indifferent to the changes and works in the same steady way that he had done under Jones.

The Meeting

Sunday is a day off for everyone. Breakfast is an hour later than usual and after this the animals ceremoniously hoist the Animal Farm flag. They then gather in the big barn for the Meeting, where they plan the work for the coming week and put forward resolutions for discussion. Only the pigs put forward resolutions as the other animals can never think of their own. Napoleon and Snowball always seem to be in opposition. The Meeting ends with the singing of 'Beasts of England' and the afternoon is for leisure.

Education for the many

The pigs learn human skills and start to organise committees and classes. Most of these projects fail, except for the reading and writing classes. By autumn, all animals are partially literate but most of them struggle. Because some of the less able animals cannot learn the Seven Commandments, Snowball summarises Animalism into the essential principle, 'Four legs good, two legs bad'. This is inscribed on the barn wall above the Seven Commandments in bigger letters.

Education for the few

Napoleon takes no notice of Snowball's committees and classes. He thinks it is a waste of time trying to educate the older animals. Instead, he takes nine puppies away to educate them himself. He keeps them in seclusion above the harness room which has become the pigs' adopted headquarters.

DO IT!

What is Orwell suggesting about the importance of education? Why does Snowball want the animals to read and write?

STRETCH IT!

Consider how the animals' inability to read and write is used against them.

Brain rations

Food is shared, except the milk, which is put into the pigs' food. When the apples begin to fall, the animals assume that these will be shared out equally. However, the pigs say the apples should be collected for their sole use also. Some animals are uneasy about this. Squealer is sent out to explain the reasoning behind the decision. He argues that it is not selfishness on the part of the pigs, but a duty for them to consume the milk and apples in order to be able to carry out their brainwork effectively for the good of all the animals on the farm. He concludes by saying that if the pigs were unable to carry out their work effectively, the consequence would be Jones's return. Everyone agrees that no one would want that.

How Orwell presents education

Snowball and Napoleon are both passionate about education. Orwell lists which animals can read (and their ability level) to show the range of outcomes that result from the same education. Of course, simply learning to read is not enough. There has to be a use for the skill. The animals are given the Seven Commandments to read to ensure they understand what Animalism is all about. This helps to ensure they work together for the common good. The pigs make use of books from the farmhouse to teach themselves about blacksmithing, carpentry and other skills. This appears to be to serve their own interests and does not prove of immediate use. Muriel the goat chooses to read scraps of newspaper from the rubbish heap and Mollie chooses to learn the letters of her own name. So far, reading seems to serve no purpose for the majority of animals. Benjamin is capable of reading but says there is nothing worth reading. Is Orwell saying education is a waste of time on Animal Farm?

Snowball wants all animals to access Animalism and invents the slogan, 'Four legs good, two legs bad!'. He is determined to help all animals to understand, which shows his desire for true equality. However, Napoleon focuses on the education of future generations. This implies he wants to focus on the young, perhaps because he can fully indoctrinate them. In contrast to Snowball's inclusiveness, by educating some and not others, Napoleon is creating more inequality.

STRETCH IT!

Do the higher levels of literacy amongst the animals always correspond with higher levels of power? Consider Muriel and Benjamin, Boxer, Clover and the pigs.

AQA exam-style question

What ideas about the power of the written word does Orwell explore in the novel *Animal Farm*?

Write about:

- how Orwell introduces examples of the written word throughout the narrative

- how Orwell presents these ideas by the ways he writes.

[30 marks]

Character and theme essentials

Boxer

Boxer's strength is impressive. It is clear that he is essential for the progress of the farm. He is described as being like three horses and almost entirely responsible for the hard labour that has to be done every day. **Structurally**, Orwell places his description of Boxer's hard work before his description of the other animals' contributions, representing his importance. The others are described as working as hard as they can and are inspired to do so because of Boxer's example.

The strength of this working-class character is respected and valued by all. His physical strength is **juxtaposed** with the intelligence of the pigs, who do no physical work.

> Orwell shows how the working class is essential to the success of Animal Farm. Boxer's devotion to the cause is impressive.

Boxer's efforts are admirable but Orwell suggests that such physical work will take over his life.

> "Boxer was the admiration of everybody. He had been a hard worker even in Jones's time, but now he seemed more like three horses than one; there were days when the entire work of the farm seemed to rest on his mighty shoulders. From morning to night he was pushing and pulling, always at the spot where the work was hardest. He had made an arrangement with one of the cockerels to call him in the mornings half an hour earlier than anyone else, and would put in some volunteer labour at whatever seemed to be most needed, before the regular day's work began. His answer to every problem, every setback, was 'I will work harder!'– which he had adopted as his personal motto."

Boxer believes that hard work will overcome all obstacles but this blinds him to the inequalities that are beginning to creep into Animal Farm.

Napoleon and Snowball

Orwell uses Snowball and Napoleon to demonstrate what happens in political debate. The conflict between the leaders foreshadows the idea that establishing equality is very difficult when the leaders do not work together.

Orwell juxtaposes Snowball and Napoleon to show the conflict in leadership. Although both are 'active in debates', the complete lack of agreement implies that the debates make slow progress. This is worrying as leaders need to work together for the greater good, not just focus on their own ideas. Orwell's use of **imagery** – 'a stormy debate' – implies trouble is brewing and foreshadows dangerous conflict between the two pigs. Orwell suggests leaders are often selfish and focused on seizing power from each other, rather than working together for the benefit of all.

Power and corruption

Napoleon and Snowball continue to be powerful agents of change. They do not need to punish or threaten the animals as they do not steal and work hard. They seem to have established rules that benefit all. However, despite their supposed dedication to the cause, the pigs now have their own headquarters (the harness room – indicating control) and do not work as part of the labour force. Although debates are held, these two pigs dominate and argue with each other rather than encouraging all animals to participate. We see that power is starting to corrupt and that these two pigs are working towards their own versions of Animalism, not necessarily for the greater good.

DO IT!

1 How does Orwell compare and contrast Napoleon, Snowball and Boxer?

2 What does he suggest about power?

REVIEW IT!

1 How can you tell the animals are happy working to gather the harvest?

2 Who is the admiration of everybody?

3 Why is Mollie's attitude to work different from that of the other animals?

4 What is Benjamin's attitude to their new way of life?

5 Why is Sunday special?

6 What is on the flag? What does this represent?

7 Who dominates the debates?

8 Name three of the committees set up by Snowball.

9 Complete the quotation, 'Four legs good, _____!'

10 Who can read just as well as the pigs but chooses not to?

11 Who does Napoleon educate in private?

12 What happens to the milk and apples? Who tells the animals?

13 Why are the birds upset?

14 How are Napoleon and Snowball similar? How are they different? Why is this significant?

15 What signs are there that the animals are not equal on Animal Farm?

16 How does Orwell show the differences in literacy levels between the animals?

17 Which books are the pigs reading? Why are they significant?

18 Where do the pigs gather in the evenings? Why?

19 It could be suggested that Napoleon is the most secretive and dangerous character in this chapter. Why?

20 At this point in the novel, to what extent could Animal Farm be said to be a success? Write a paragraph explaining your thoughts.

Chapter 4

Propaganda wars

DO IT!

What is Orwell suggesting about the effects of the Rebellion on other animals beyond the farm? Why are the farmers scared?

STRETCH IT!

Using the events of the Russian October and February Revolutions as an example (see page 72), consider whether a similar Animal-Farm style rebellion would be able to succeed. What factors would influence its success/failure?

Summary

By late summer, news of the Rebellion has spread via the tune of 'Beasts of England' and by the pigeons. Jones spends his time in the local pub, complaining. The other farmers (Pilkington and Frederick) do not offer to help and instead secretly wonder how they might benefit from Jones's misfortune. The two farmers are rivals but are both concerned that their own animals may rebel. They try to counteract the pigs' propaganda pigeons by predicting the failure of the farm, saying the animals will starve, and then spread rumours that the animals are uncivilised cannibals and insane. However, the animals on neighbouring farms do not fully believe the stories the farmers tell and begin small-scale rebellions of their own. The farmers are scared.

Through Pilkington and Frederick, Orwell is exploring the role of other countries' reactions to the Russian Revolution (see pages 71–74).

Battle of the Cowshed

On 12 October, Jones and his men and half a dozen others from neighbouring farms come to recapture the farm. Jones carries a gun and the rest carry sticks. Snowball has been reading about defensive strategy used by Julius Caesar and has prepared the animals for such an action. Snowball launches a series of attacks. All of the animals fight bravely especially Snowball and Boxer. A sheep is killed. Boxer fears he has killed a stable boy and is full of remorse but Snowball tells him not to feel sentimental. Mollie is found hiding in the barn. The animals celebrate their victory and have a memorial service for the dead sheep. Snowball and Boxer are awarded 'Animal Hero, First Class' and the dead sheep is named 'Animal Hero, Second Class'. They agree to call the battle 'Battle of the Cowshed' and place Jones's gun at the foot of the flagstaff to be fired on the anniversary of this battle and on Midsummer Day for the anniversary of the Rebellion.

A war of words

Orwell shows the pigs' desire to spread Animalism beyond Animal Farm. The farmers' fear is that their own animals will be inspired to rebel against them. The pigeons infiltrate the neighbouring animals and share the story of Animal Farm's success and teach them the song 'Beasts of England'. Several significant rebellions occur. This implies that propaganda is a powerful way by which political messages can be spread. Interestingly, we do not know exactly what the pigeons tell the animals on other farms so have no way of verifying if their information is accurate. Do we assume that Napoleon and Snowball would be truthful when promoting Animalism? Perhaps this is as foolish as assuming our own governments would never lie to us about the reality of life in our country.

Fear among the farmers

When words fail, both Frederick and Pilkington resort to violence as a method of control. After several small-scale rebellions and the astonishing spread of 'Beasts of England', the farmers beat animals who sing the song. Orwell depicts universal cruelty among leaders who fear losing control. The farmers' actions mirror those of Jones that led to the original rebellion. Pilkington and Frederick also allow their men to join Jones when he attempts to retake the farm, but do not participate themselves. We can see that the farmers are scared to directly challenge the leaders of Animal Farm. However, because of their rivalry, they fail to unite forces against their common enemy. Orwell portrays the farmers' fear that their own animals will rebel. They counteract the pigs' propaganda with their own shocking misinformation. Rumours of 'terrible wickedness' and 'cannibalism' are spread.

DEFINE IT!

propaganda – the use of news, media, music and art to spread biased political messages; usually used by governments and political leaders

Metaphor to show they change tactics

Emotive language

"Frederick and Pilkington changed their tune and began to talk of the terrible wickedness that now flourished on Animal Farm…cannibalism, tortured one another with red-hot horseshoes, and had their females in common."

Listing of the awful allegations

This shows how the farmers attempt to use fear to encourage their animals to remain enslaved. This tactic is largely unsuccessful but Orwell nevertheless wants us to consider the source of our news and the motivations of those who use information to control populations. This use of propaganda by both pigs and humans shows their similarity: both those inside and outside Animal Farm recognise the power of propaganda. Orwell is exposing how leaders use such methods to control their populations and influence the working class.

AQA exam-style question

How does Orwell portray ideas about leadership in the novel *Animal Farm*?

Write about:

- how Orwell introduces ideas about leadership throughout the narrative

- how Orwell presents these ideas by the ways he writes.

[30 marks]

Character and theme essentials

Snowball the hero

Snowball's emergence as a committed and capable leader proves how easily he could seize power from Napoleon. Napoleon and Squealer are noticeably absent during and after the battle, which implies they are cowards, just like Mollie. This momentous battle has divided the pigs and is a victory for Snowball in more ways than one. His achievements are recognised by the other animals and at the sheep's funeral, Snowball's short speech recognises the need for 'all animals to be ready to die for Animal Farm'. Such commitment to the cause is admirable. His lack of compassion for the human victim is interesting to consider and juxtaposes with Boxer's reaction. Snowball asserts, 'War is war. The only good human being is a dead one.' This chilling statement strongly implies Snowball would never work with humans or behave like a human in future.

DO IT!

Here a student is writing about the bravery of Snowball.

> Orwell depicts Snowball as an intelligent and brave leader. His decision to head straight for Jones, who is carrying a gun, shows his dedication to the cause of Animalism. He is willing to sacrifice his life for the greater good of the farm and the animals unite behind him and follow every order. His courage sets him apart from the other pigs. This establishes him as a more effective leader than Napoleon. When Snowball and Boxer are given the military decoration 'Animal Hero, First Class' as thanks for their outstanding contributions, it is clear that the animals recognise and reward such commitment to the cause.

Explain briefly to what extent you agree with this student's view of the significance of Snowball's bravery in the battle. What is Orwell suggesting about leadership?

Boxer and the stable boy

Boxer's impressive performance in the battle culminates in him kicking a stable boy in the head, 'striking out'. He is wearing iron shoes and the boy appears to be dead. After the humans have been chased from the farm, Boxer is full of remorse: 'I had no intention of doing that'. Boxer is full of compassion, even for the human enemy, which encourages us to sympathise with Boxer and shows the suffering of those who are forced to fight to defend their own country. Boxer tries to turn the boy over, 'pawing with his hoof'. The verbs 'striking' and 'pawing' show the two sides of Boxer, who is immensely capable of causing damage but who is also kind and caring. He is rewarded with the same decoration as Snowball, again showing that Animal Farm is only successful because of the collaborative efforts of great leaders and great workers.

STRETCH IT!

Re-read the account of the battle. How does Snowball use strategic methods to defend the farm? Do the animals work well together? Is there any risk Jones will win? What does this suggest about Snowball's leadership?

Leadership

Orwell portrays Snowball as an excellent leader: strong, intelligent and dedicated to protecting the farm and its inhabitants. Napoleon's absence implies he is neither threat nor use in times of crisis or when there is a need to plan for the future. Although Snowball leads the animals, they work collaboratively and make unanimous decisions, such as to confer medals on Boxer and Snowball. Boxer is also presented as a leader, both in battle and at work. The animals need such role models to inspire and motivate them. Perhaps Orwell is suggesting that is the true purpose of a leader.

REVIEW IT!

1   How do animals on other farms learn the song 'Beasts of England'?

2   Where has Jones been spending his time?

3   Who are the two neighbouring farmers? What are their farms called?

4   What unites these two farmers?

5   What rumours do the farmers spread about the animals of Animal Farm?

6   What name do the farmers use for Animal Farm?

7   When does the Battle of the Cowshed begin?

8   How many men does Jones bring with him?

9   Snowball's defensive strategy is inspired by his study of which great leader?

10   Which animals take part in the first line of the attack? What do they do?

11   Which animals take part in the second line of the attack? What do they do?

12   Who does Snowball charge at?

13   Snowball is bleeding by the end of the battle. Why?

14   Who is the most terrifying animal in battle? Why?

15   Why are the animals taking so much pleasure in attacking the humans?

16   How does Orwell show Boxer as remorseful?

17   Which animal dies in the battle?

18   Where is Mollie during the battle? Why?

19   Three military decorations are awarded. Who receives them, and why?

20   The animals successfully defend their farm. What does this suggest about the future of Animal Farm? Write a paragraph explaining your thoughts.

Chapter 5

Snowball versus Napoleon

Summary

Mollie becomes lazier. She is seen with one of Pilkington's men and Clover discovers she has been hiding sugar and ribbons. Three days later, she disappears. The pigeons see her in the nearby village working for the humans.

The weather in January is harsh. Snowball and Napoleon compete for power. Snowball develops plans for a windmill to provide electricity and reduce workload. He draws his plans on the floor of the shed. Napoleon urinates on them. The animals are divided over who to support. Snowball promises a three-day week; Napoleon promises a full manger. Napoleon wants to buy weapons; Snowball wants to use the pigeons to encourage rebellions on other farms.

Napoleon seizes power

The animals gather for their weekly Meeting and debate the windmill. Snowball's speech is impressive but Napoleon uses his army of dogs to chase him away. The animals are shocked; some of the pigs protest but are scared into silence by the dogs.

Napoleon's use of his dog army is presented by Orwell to satirise the ways in which political opponents are eliminated.

The dogs are presented as powerful, aggressive and well trained. Their collars show they are owned by Napoleon and under his control. They represent his aggression and violent side.

The dogs have been trained to attack Snowball. This shows the attack has been planned and suggests that leaders plot to remove rivals.

> "…nine enormous dogs wearing brass-studded collars came bounding into the barn. They dashed straight for Snowball, who only sprang from his place just in time to escape their snapping jaws. In a moment he was out of the door and they were after him. Too amazed and frightened to speak, all the animals crowded through the door to watch the chase.

The animals' reaction shows they are united in horror but powerless to defend Snowball, despite their loyalty to him. Orwell shows the population is powerless against ruthless, violent dictators.

DO IT!

What is Orwell suggesting about the use of fear to control populations? Is Napoleon a good leader?

Napoleon announces that there will be no more debates at the Meetings. Instead, decisions will be made by a committee of pigs. The animals will still assemble on Sundays to salute the flag, sing 'Beasts of England' and receive orders. Squealer persuades the animals that this is for the best. Old Major's skull is placed at the foot of the flag beside a gun for the animals to file past as they enter the Meeting. Napoleon changes his mind about the windmill and announces that it will be built after all. Squealer tells all the animals privately that the windmill had been Napoleon's idea all along and that Snowball was a traitor who had stolen Napoleon's plans.

Intelligence versus violence

Snowball's strengths as a leader are his ability to innovate and his intellectual power. Napoleon urinates on Snowball's drawings which shows his disgust but it also shows his inability to think of a better plan or explain his objections. They also disagree on the question of defence. Napoleon sees weapons as essential for their future survival but Snowball believes that if the Rebellion spreads there will be no need.

When they debate, Snowball is so eloquent and inspirational that it seems certain the animals will vote for the windmill and Snowball. Napoleon uses his personal army (the dogs) to chase Snowball off the farm. This shows Napoleon feels insecure about his position of power.

It is ironic that Napoleon later decides to build Snowball's windmill. This calculated move shows he is aware of the scheme's popularity and actually agrees with it himself. Again we see the use of propaganda as history is rewritten to suit Napoleon's narrative.

End of Animalism

Orwell's narrative takes a dark turn when Napoleon uses his army to chase his rival Snowball out of Animal Farm. It is significant as this is the end of the golden era of Animalism and it is clear that this marks the beginning of his tyrannical rule of terror and bloodshed.

 AQA exam-style question

How does Orwell use the character of Napoleon to explore ideas about propaganda in *Animal Farm*?

Write about:

* what Napoleon's actions reveal about truth and manipulation throughout the novel

* how Orwell presents Napoleon.

[30 marks]

Character and theme essentials

Snowball the banished intellectual

DO IT!

How is Orwell suggesting Animalism is over?

What has been lost from old Major's vision?

Snowball's expulsion represents the end of hope for the animals. They are now at the mercy of Napoleon. You can see that the other animals are unlikely or unable to challenge Napoleon, especially when faced with the threat of violence and the return of Jones. Snowball escapes with his life but only just; this is the moment when freedom of speech, debate and the hopes and dreams of Animalism come to a violent end.

Napoleon and dictatorship

Napoleon now has complete control over the farm. He is not committed to the idea of equality and appears power hungry, aggressive and controlling. He is now far more powerful than any other animal. His calm and cold performance in the barn shows that he had planned his attack on Snowball and feels no remorse. What will become of the animals now? Napoleon maintains order by instilling fear in the population. He removes the animals' right to debate and express their opinions. The Sunday Meetings are now a time when they are given orders. In effect, Napoleon creates a dictatorship overnight, which he maintains through fear (dogs) and the obedience of the masses (his mindless sheep bleating on command).

STRETCH IT!

Compare old Major's description of human tyrannical rule with that of Napoleon. What do you notice? How far can Napoleon be compared with Stalin?

Squealer and propaganda

Squealer's role becomes more significant as the novel progresses. He is a vital tool in Napoleon's regime. His spread of misinformation, fearmongering and propaganda ensures that discontent is addressed within the population and the animals are manipulated. His repeated rhetorical question, 'Surely, comrades, you do not want Jones back?' is used to silence protest. This threat inspires fear and makes the animals more willing to believe his lies. Boxer and the others no longer trust their own memories and rely on what Squealer presents as truth. We might say the animals oppress themselves through their refusal to challenge Squealer and his version of the truth.

REVIEW IT!

1 Who leaves the farm by choice? Why?

2 Who is expelled from the farm? Why? What does this represent?

3 How does Napoleon react to Snowball's plan for a windmill?

4 What are the two slogans used by Snowball and Napoleon?

5 What is the main purpose of the windmill? What does it represent?

6 Why is the windmill popular with the animals?

7 Where does Snowball draw his plans?

8 How long does Snowball say it will take to build the windmill?

9 How long does Napoleon say it will take to build the windmill?

10 What does Napoleon want to do to defend the farm?

11 What does Snowball want to do to defend the farm?

12 Who speaks for around thirty seconds at the Meeting?

13 Why is Snowball's speech impressive?

14 Who are the nine animals wearing collars?

15 What almost happens to Snowball? What does this represent?

16 How does Orwell portray Napoleon as superior to the other animals?

17 What will no longer take place on Sundays?

18 Who objects to what Napoleon has done?

19 What is the name of the pig who writes poems and songs?

20 The animals now live in fear of Napoleon. What does this suggest about the future of Animal Farm? Write a paragraph explaining your thoughts.

Chapter 6

Overcoming obstacles

Summary

All year, the animals work very hard to build the windmill. They do 60-hour weeks and Napoleon says they can 'volunteer' to work Sundays. However, if they don't volunteer, their rations are reduced by half. They break up the boulders by rolling them up to the top of the quarry and then smashing them by pushing them over the edge. Although they have most of the necessary materials available on the farm, the animals realise they will have to trade to get things such as oil, nails and string. The animals are uneasy about this and have to be persuaded by Squealer. Napoleon hires Whymper, a human lawyer, to help them trade with other farms. Whymper will visit the farm every Monday to meet with the pigs. Napoleon wants to sell hay, wheat and perhaps eggs. Napoleon is now addressed as 'Leader'.

The pigs move into the farmhouse, sleep in beds and eat in the kitchen. This breaks the Fourth Commandment. The animals are upset by this and Clover takes Muriel to the barn to help her read. The commandment has been changed to 'No animal shall sleep in a bed *with sheets*'. Squealer persuades them that this is essential for the pigs' wellbeing. He asks, 'Surely none of you wishes to see Jones back?' Some days afterwards it is announced that the pigs will now get up an hour later than the other animals.

In November, a horrendous storm comes and the windmill is destroyed. Napoleon says Snowball is to blame and pronounces a death sentence upon him. Napoleon offers a reward of 'Animal Hero, Second Class' for any animal that can capture Snowball alive and insists they will rebuild the windmill all through the winter.

The division of labour

The windmill is the animals' sole focus. The majority work very long hours to build this structure based on Snowball's plans but under Napoleon's leadership. Boxer's strength may be impressive but his blind devotion to Napoleon is concerning. He works his 60-hour week, plus an extra three hours 45 minutes each week, as well as extra night work. His Herculean power seems to be driven by a devotion that prevents him questioning leadership. The irony is that Boxer is working for the benefit of the pigs. Napoleon's tyrannical leadership involves the animals working excessively hard while the pigs reap the rewards.

Squealer's use of **rhetorical devices** and devious wordplay is very effective. Look at how he convinces the animals it is right that the pigs sleep in beds.

> Orwell shows Squealer using rhetorical questions and direct address to challenge them. By addressing them as comrades, Squealer pretends to be one of them and acting in their best interests.

"
'You have heard then, comrades,' he said, 'that we pigs now sleep in the beds of the farmhouse? And why not? You did not suppose, surely, that there was ever a ruling against *beds*? A bed merely means a place to sleep in. A pile of straw in a stall is a bed, properly regarded. The rule was against *sheets*, which are a human invention. We have removed the sheets from the farmhouse beds, and sleep between blankets.'
"

> Squealer's redefinition of 'bed' and rewriting of the commandment allows the pigs to seize privileges. Orwell suggests that the animals are easily persuaded, which foreshadows greater inequality.

AQA exam-style question

How does Orwell portray ideas about equality in the novel *Animal Farm*?

Write about:

- how Orwell introduces ideas about equality throughout the narrative

- how Orwell presents these ideas by the ways he writes.

[30 marks]

DO IT!

1 Why is this first amendment of the commandments so significant? What is suggested about the power of the written word?

2 Re-read the commandments in full. Which are changed or broken, by whom and when? What do you notice about the irony of some of these statements when you consider life on Animal Farm under Napoleon's leadership?

Character and theme essentials

Napoleon the Leader and class divide

Orwell has previously described Napoleon's selfishness and willingness to ignore the principles of Animalism that he does not support. Compare his actions with old Major's principles set out in his speech in Chapter 1 and the Seven Commandments established in Chapter 2. It is clear that two classes of animals have been created: the pigs and the other animals.

DO IT!

Complete the table with examples of the animals acting against old Major's principles/the Seven Commandments since Napoleon seizes power in Chapter 5. One has been done for you.

Principle/commandment	After Napoleon seizes power in Chapter 5
'No animal must ever live in a house, or sleep in a bed'	The pigs move into the farmhouse and sleep in human beds, with blankets. Napoleon re-writes the fourth commandment to 'No animal shall sleep in a bed with sheets.'
'No animal must…ever engage in trade'	
'No animal shall kill any other animal'	
'All animals are equal'	

We need to pay attention to how Napoleon has gradually changed the shape and content of the weekly Meetings, formerly a place for lively debate. He is always accompanied by his personal army (the dogs) and uses Squealer to spread propaganda supporting Napoleon's decisions. Squealer now also gets the animals to question their own memories. When the animals try to think for themselves (Clover reading the commandments), he uses their blind faith in the written word to control them. This rewriting of history is blatantly obvious but the animals apparently continue to trust Napoleon as their leader. Napoleon is now also giving human lawyer Whymper orders too. This both impresses and concerns the animals.

Hopes and dreams: the windmill

The windmill project represents the hopes and dreams of the animals for a life with less hard work. It is also a reminder of Snowball's intelligence and vision. Its destruction is blamed on Snowball but is this true? The destruction of the windmill parallels the destruction of the principle of Animalism.

REVIEW IT!

1 How many hours a week do most animals have to work?

2 Who works the hardest? What does this mean about equality on the farm?

3 Why is building the windmill so challenging?

4 What system do the animals use to speed up the process?

5 Who is Whymper and how is he connected to Napoleon?

6 Which seven things are the animals short of that cannot be produced on the farm?

7 What does Napoleon intend to sell?

8 What does Squealer say about trade with humans that is a lie?

9 What is Napoleon's new title?

10 What do the pigs now sleep in?

11 Which animals re-read the commandments?

12 What has happened to the Fourth Commandment?

13 Which animals get up an hour later each day?

14 Who completes extra work at night?

15 What happens to the windmill on the night of the storm?

16 Who does Napoleon blame?

17 What reward does Napoleon offer and why?

18 What does Napoleon say must be done about the windmill?

19 What is the name of the pig with a thunderous voice?

20 The animals have worked so hard on the windmill only to have it destroyed. What does this suggest about the future of Animal Farm? Write a paragraph explaining your thoughts.

Chapter 7

A hard winter

Summary

Winter is challenging and the animals work hard rebuilding the windmill. By January, they are struggling to survive but are still inspired by Boxer's hard work. The animals are starving but Napoleon keeps this secret from the other farmers. Rumours are spread by the other farmers that the animals are cannibals and commit infanticide. Napoleon uses Whymper, the lawyer, to spread an opposing rumour by taking him on a tour of the farm and showing off his 'huge' stores of food, which are actually bins filled with sand with a little grain on top. Napoleon stays in the farmhouse guarded by his dog army and issues his orders via Squealer.

The hens revolt

The hens are told to surrender their eggs. They attempt a protest by flying to the rafters to lay their eggs, where they fall and smash. The hens' revolt is doomed. No other animals support the hens' cause. After death, they are buried without ceremony; cause of death is concealed.

Orwell shows an attempt by the working class to rebel against the leadership. The protest is in keeping with the principles of Animalism; we are encouraged to sympathise with the hens.

> "For the first time since the expulsion of Jones, there was something resembling a rebellion. Led by three young Black Minorca pullets, the hens made a determined effort to thwart Napoleon's wishes. Their method was to fly up to the rafters and there lay their eggs, which smashed to pieces on the floor. Napoleon acted swiftly and ruthlessly. He ordered the hens' rations to be stopped, and decreed that any animal giving so much as a grain of corn to a hen should be punished by death. The dogs saw to it that these orders were carried out. For five days the hens held out, then they capitulated and went back to their nesting boxes. Nine hens had died in the meantime. Their bodies were buried in the orchard, and it was given out that they had died of coccidiosis."

Napoleon's response is to eliminate the opposition. As he is in charge of the food supply, it is easy to end their Rebellion.

Although several hens are willing to die, the Rebellion is brought under control quickly and the truth about events is suppressed: the animals must follow orders without question, or lose their lives.

Napoleon pursues trade deals with the other farmers. One plan is to sell the hens' eggs. You need to consider whether such trade was inevitable.

Snowball the secret agent

Snowball is made the scapegoat for all issues on the farm. He allegedly sneaks on to the farm at night to cause damage and disruption. He is also accused of selling himself to Frederick of Pinchfield Farm and of plotting an attack. Squealer tells the animals that Snowball was Jones's secret agent all along. Boxer challenges this but Squealer persuades him by saying there is written evidence which the animals could see for themselves if they could read. Squealer uses false memories to convince the animals that Snowball was a traitor and that in fact there are other secret agents among them.

The terror of the purges

Four days later, Napoleon gathers the animals in the yard. His dogs attack four pigs and try to attack Boxer. The pigs are forced to confess to being in league with Snowball and to having arranged to hand Animal Farm over to Frederick. They also confirm that Snowball had confessed to being Jones's secret agent. The dogs savagely kill them. Next, three hens, a goose, three sheep and many other animals confess to crimes. The dogs kill them all. The bodies pile up.

The remaining animals are shocked and scared. They huddle on the knoll. Boxer reacts by saying he will work harder and goes off to the quarry. Clover remembers old Major's optimistic vision and feels that Animal Farm has fallen short of that vision. The animals sing 'Beasts of England' but are stopped by Squealer, who tells them the song is now banned.

The horrific, bloody and public executions in the yard not only break the Sixth Commandment ('No animal shall kill any other animal.') but appear to have been planned and implemented to intimidate and control the animals. The animals watch four pigs confess to being in league with Snowball. They are torn apart by the dogs. After this, many other animals confess to strange crimes perhaps due to mass hysteria and panic. Napoleon's regime has become deeply disturbing.

Orwell shows Napoleon is prepared to murder any animal that stands in his way. He will not tolerate any form of protest or dissent: he is portrayed as a ruthless dictator who will stop at nothing to get his own way.

DO IT!

The animals are now struggling to survive. Write a list of factors that make life on Animal Farm very challenging.

STRETCH IT!

Consider the impact of this ongoing suffering on the animals' morale. How do the animals cope with the pressure (or fail to cope)? Examine the reactions of Boxer and Clover. Which methods does Orwell use to portray their suffering (for example, speech, action, reaction)?

AQA exam-style question

How does Orwell portray ideas about protest and rebellion in the novel *Animal Farm*? How is the novel a critique of the Russian Revolution and its consequences?

Write about:

- how Orwell introduces ideas about protest and rebellion throughout the narrative

- how Orwell presents these ideas by the ways he writes.

[30 marks]

DOIT!

Squealer is rewriting the history of Animal Farm. What stops the other animals challenging his version of events? What is Orwell suggesting about powerful leadership and propaganda? Write a paragraph with evidence to support your answer.

Character and theme essentials

Squealer the propaganda machine

Squealer is essentially the only means of contact between the animals and Napoleon. Napoleon uses him to make announcements and spread misinformation. He is both the bringer of bad news and crusher of potential challenges. Squealer is used to demand the hens give up their eggs for sale. The hens' rebellion shows Squealer's propaganda is losing its power.

Snowball the scapegoat

Snowball is depicted as Jones's secret agent, which seems absurd given how bravely he fought in the Battle of the Cowshed. However, Squealer convinces the animals of Snowball's guilt using false memories and reference to written evidence. This rewriting of history shows the extent to which propaganda can effectively eliminate truth from historical records.

Hopes and dreams: the death of Animalism

When Clover reflects with sadness on all they have lost, she is mourning the loss of their hopes and dreams. Orwell portrays her leading the animals in singing 'Beasts of England', slowly and sadly to reflect this loss. Squealer tells the animals that 'Beasts of England' has been banned as the Revolution is over and the vision is no longer relevant. He asserts that a better society has been established and introduces the new song (composed by Minimus) 'Animal Farm, Animal Farm' which ironically opens with 'Never through me shalt thou come to harm!' No one dares to protest. This marks the death of the dream of Animalism.

STRETCHIT!

Boxer is the only animal who confronts Squealer's lies. Consider how Boxer is portrayed throughout this chapter as:

a a very hard worker

b an inspiration

c a challenge to Squealer/Napoleon's authority

d an animal capable of destroying Napoleon's army

e a fool who cannot accept the reality of Napoleon's tyrannical rule.

Find examples to support your answer.

REVIEW IT!

1 The animals are rebuilding the windmill. What change have they made to the design?

2 Who is an inspiration to the other animals?

3 What are the animals short of?

4 What two things are the animals accused of by the other farmers?

5 How does Napoleon use Whymper to spread positive propaganda?

6 Why do the hens protest? Why is this significant?

7 How does the protest end?

8 Who wants to buy the pile of timber?

9 Who is the farm's scapegoat?

10 Squealer tells the animals a new history of the Battle of the Cowshed. What is different?

11 Why does Boxer challenge Squealer?

12 What persuades Boxer he is wrong?

13 Which animals do the dogs attack first? Why?

14 Who is attacked second and defends himself?

15 What do the other animals confess to?

16 Where do the remaining animals go because they are scared?

17 What does Clover remember about old Major's vision?

18 How does Clover feel about the past and the present?

19 Clover has lots of thoughts. Why can't she express them?

20 The animals sing 'Beasts of England' to comfort themselves. What do you notice about the way it is sung and what happens as a consequence? Write a paragraph explaining your thoughts.

Chapter 8

Rewritten rules

Summary

The animals find the Sixth Commandment has been rewritten to say, 'No animals shall kill any other animal *without cause*.' The animals work harder than ever before and food is scarce. Squealer reports that food production is up but the animals do not feel the benefit. Napoleon is seen less and less in public. He now lives in his own part of the farmhouse and is becoming god-like; he is given credit for every success and stroke of luck. Minimus, the poet pig, composes a poem in Napoleon's honour, which is written on the barn wall. Squealer paints Napoleon's portrait (in white paint) above the poem. However, not all of the animals love him. In the middle of the summer, three hens confess to plotting to kill Napoleon. They are executed and new measures for Napoleon's protection are put in place.

Timber trades

Napoleon negotiates with both Frederick and Pilkington about selling the pile of timber. Both farmers become enemies and allies at different stages of the negotiations. The pigeons are used to spread propaganda.

Rumours

Rumours are rife about an impending attack from Frederick and Snowball's continuing malevolent actions. A gander confesses to witnessing Snowball mixing weed seed with seed corn and then commits suicide. It is claimed that Snowball had never received the order of 'Animal Hero, First Class' and that he'd actually been a coward in the Battle of the Cowshed. The animals are again bewildered by this but Squealer convinces them that they have misremembered events. The animals exert huge efforts to gather the harvest and complete the windmill. Napoleon names the windmill Napoleon Mill. Two days later, Napoleon announces that he had been in secret agreement with Frederick all along and has now sold the wood to him. Relations with Foxwood are broken off. Insulting messages are sent to Pilkington. Napoleon assures the animals that the rumours of Frederick's attack were untrue and that rumours of his cruelty were wildly exaggerated and the invention of Snowball and his agents. Once the timber has all been collected, Napoleon calls a meeting displaying the pile of cash he's received for it. Three days later, Whymper races to the farm to tell Napoleon that Frederick's banknotes are forgeries. An attack on the farm by Frederick and his men is expected at any moment. The pigeons are sent to Foxwood Farm to try to get Pilkington back on side but he sends the message back, 'Serves you right.'

Battle of the Windmill

The next morning, Frederick and his men attack the farm and blow up the windmill. A bloody battle follows. The animals win but many are killed and wounded. After the men flee, Squealer comes out of the farmhouse in triumph. Napoleon makes a rousing speech and two days are given over for celebrations. The battle is named the Battle of the Windmill and Napoleon awards himself 'Order of the Green Banner'. The banknote forgery is forgotten.

A few days later, the pigs find whisky in the cellar and get very drunk. The next day the pigs are very hungover. Napoleon is said to be dying and there is a rumour that Snowball has poisoned his food. However, Napoleon recovers and instructs Whymper to buy books to learn how to make alcohol and has a small paddock ploughed to grow barley. Around this time, Squealer is found late one night sprawled beside the Seven Commandments with a tin of white paint and a paintbrush. The Fifth Commandment has been changed to 'No animal shall drink alcohol *to excess*.'

Trading with humans

Napoleon tries to outsmart his rival farmers by negotiating trade deals with both. He plays them off against each other in order to get a higher price for the timber. He uses his pigeon propaganda machine to spread the slogan 'Death to Frederick' then alters this to 'Death to Pilkington'. Both farmers are accused of working with Snowball to destroy Animal Farm. Eventually, he sells the timber to Frederick and the money is supposed to pay for the machinery for the windmill.

Unfortunately, by playing these games, Napoleon ends up with a pile of forged banknotes, no timber and two enemies. The trade deals were driven by greed and Orwell shows that Napoleon's desire to behave like a human capitalist leader results in a serious loss for Animal Farm. In addition, it can be argued that his behaviour leads to Frederick's decision to attack the farm and destroy the windmill. At this point, Pilkington sends a note saying 'Serves you right'. Not only has Animal Farm lost out financially as a result of Napoleon's poor judgement, but animals lose their lives in the battle and lose hope for future prosperity (symbolised by the windmill). Napoleon Mill was supposed to represent Napoleon's successful leadership. Instead, it represents his failings.

AQA exam-style question

How does Orwell portray ideas about conflict between leaders in the novel *Animal Farm*?

Write about:

- how Orwell introduces ideas about conflict between leaders throughout the narrative

- how Orwell presents these ideas by the ways he writes.

[30 marks]

DO IT!

The Battle of the Windmill is brutal. Compare the injuries and deaths from this battle with The Battle of the Cowshed. What are the similarities and what are the differences between the two battles?

 ## STRETCH IT!

How does Orwell portray Napoleon's leadership during and after the Battle of the Windmill? What is similar to and different from the way Snowball led the animals in the Battle of the Cowshed? What point is Orwell making about leadership?

Character and theme essentials

Napoleon's god-like status

Napoleon's superiority is clear. He separates himself from the other pigs and makes himself into a god-like figure. He has poems that celebrate his greatness, his portrait painted on the wall and many titles. By deifying himself, Napoleon ensures his decisions will go unchallenged giving him supreme power. The animals love and respect him. He can take the lives of animals at will, keep those alive who are useful and control what his population are told about life beyond the farm. His titles include 'Terror of mankind' and 'Protector of the Sheep-fold' yet he falls short in the Battle of the Windmill. Of course, the narrow victory is celebrated and Napoleon gives himself another honour.

Boxer the broken

Boxer may still be a powerful force but it is clear that he is getting old and cannot compete with such a well-armed enemy force as Frederick and his men. He is badly injured (physically) and is also mentally broken. The injuries to his knees and hooves are significant as he knows he will have to put a lot of pressure on his legs rebuilding the windmill. He reflects on his age and feels exhausted by the thought of it. Boxer seriously injures at least three men in the battle but shows no remorse this time. He has become weary and indoctrinated, believing humans can be killed without remorse as they are the enemy. When the gun is fired to celebrate the victory, Boxer expresses his frustration and depression at the destruction of the windmill. He says, 'We have won back what we had before', implying he now sees efforts to maintain Animal Farm as futile and hopeless.

Rewriting the rules

In this chapter, two commandments have been changed: the Sixth, 'No animals shall kill any other animal *without cause*', and the Fifth, 'No animal shall drink alcohol *to excess*'. Both are changed to ensure that Napoleon's appalling decisions remain 'legal' as they are in line with the law of the farm. Squealer is found in the middle of the night on the floor of the barn. There is a broken ladder and a pot of paint. Orwell states that the animals are confused by this but it is clear that this is who has been rewriting the commandments. The success of this strategy relies on the animals' collective lack of intelligence and willingness to blindly trust their leaders. Only the pigs can have other animals killed and drink alcohol.

THE SEVEN COMMANDMENTS

1. Whatever goes upon two legs is an enemy.
2. Whatever goes upon four legs, or has wings, is a freind.
3. No animal shall wear clothes.
4. No animal shall sleep in a bed.
5. No animal shall drink alcohol.
6. No animal shall kill any other animal without cause.
7. All animals are equal.

The pigs' discovery of whisky in the cellar leads to them becoming very drunk and staying in bed very late the next day. Look at how Napoleon changes his mind rapidly about the consumption of alcohol.

1 He consumes it and becomes very drunk.

2 The next day, he stays in bed claiming to be dying.

3 His 'dying' wish is that all who drink alcohol be punished by death.

4 He recovers and orders books on brewing.

5 He has the commandment changed to allow drinking to occur.

How does this represent the problems with Napoleon's leadership?

REVIEW IT!

1 What change is made to the Sixth Commandment?

2 Name four of Napoleon's new titles.

3 What is the name of the poem Minimus writes about Napoleon? What message does it convey about Napoleon?

4 What is painted on the barn wall?

5 What product is Napoleon trying to sell?

6 Why does Napoleon get Pinkeye the pig to taste his food?

7 In which season is Napoleon Mill finished?

8 When Napoleon finally receives money from trade, what is the issue with the banknotes?

9 Who does Napoleon pronounce a death sentence upon?

10 How many men does Frederick bring to the Battle of the Windmill?

11 How many guns do the men have?

12 What happens to the windmill?

13 Which animals are injured or killed?

14 How many men's heads does Boxer break?

15 Which injuries does Boxer have?

16 How old is Boxer now?

17 What do the pigs find in the cellar?

18 Why does Napoleon think he is dying?

19 What is the significance of the changes to the commandments in this chapter?

20 The animals have won another battle. They celebrate but the mood is very different. Compare the celebrations after the animals win the Battle of the Cowshed and the Battle of the Windmill. Write a paragraph explaining your thoughts.

Chapter 9

Boxer's decline

Summary

Boxer remains injured (his split hoof takes a long time to heal) but refuses to take time off work and ignores Clover and Benjamin's warning not to work so hard on the rebuilding of the windmill. He looks forward to his promised retirement on his twelfth birthday. The retirement ages had been agreed after the Rebellion but the retirement pasture is now used for growing barley.

Another hard winter

The winter is as cold as the previous year and the food supply even shorter. The animals' rations are reduced again, except for the pigs and dogs. Squealer talks of 'readjustments' rather than 'reductions' and reads out figures to prove that they are still better off today than when Jones was still in charge. The animals can no longer remember the old days well enough to disagree. They believe Squealer for after all they are no longer slaves.

Pigs' privileges

Napoleon fathers thirty-one piglets who are kept away from the other animals and schooled privately. Animals have to step aside to let pigs pass. Pigs are also given the privilege of wearing green ribbons on their tails on Sundays. The farm has a fairly good year but is still short of money. Rations are reduced again yet the pigs remain comfortable. They are allowed a pint of beer per day, with half a gallon for Napoleon.

Orwell shows how the upper-class elite (Napoleon and the pigs) lead a decadent lifestyle while the working-class animals suffer. The pigs' privilege is juxtaposed with the other animals' struggle to survive, including Boxer who is badly injured but is determined to work hard. Orwell shows that the elite are selfish and are only interested in members of their own class.

Pomp and ceremony

Napoleon demands that a Spontaneous Demonstration is held each week to celebrate the success of Animal Farm. This involves marching in military formation and poems read in his honour. Some animals complain about the time the processions take up but are drowned out by the sheep bleating 'Four legs good, two legs bad!'. Generally, the animals are glad to be distracted from their hunger and hardship.

Republic and religion

In April, Animal Farm becomes a republic and Napoleon is elected President unanimously. New documents are 'discovered' revealing more of Snowball's treachery and Napoleon's heroics in the Battle of the Cowshed.

Moses the raven returns and preaches about Sugarcandy Mountain again. The pigs say Moses is lying but they let him stay and share beer with him.

'Get out, Boxer, get out!'

Boxer's hoof heals and he works as hard as ever but is growing old. Late one summer evening, he collapses while dragging a load of stone. The animals run to get help from Squealer, who shows a lot of concern and explains that Napoleon is arranging to send Boxer to hospital. Boxer remains in his stall for the next two days. He is looking forward to retirement. However, the next day, when the animals are working in the field, Benjamin raises the alarm that a van has come to take Boxer away. The animals race to say goodbye but Benjamin furiously reads out the writing on the side of the van, 'Horse Slaughterer'. Clover shouts for Boxer to escape. Boxer tries to kick his way out but fails. Three days later, it is announced that Boxer is dead.

Squealer comes to tell the animals about Boxer's final hours.

> Orwell shows Squealer pretending to care about Boxer. His grief is faked for propaganda purposes and to give his story credibility.

> "
> 'It was the most affecting sight I have ever seen!' said Squealer, lifting his trotter and wiping away a tear. 'I was at his bedside at the very last. And at the end, almost too weak to speak, he whispered in my ear that his sole sorrow was to have passed on before the windmill was finished. "Forward, comrades!" he whispered. "Forward in the name of the Rebellion…" Those were his very last words, comrades.'
> "

> Squealer explains that Boxer was devoted to Animal Farm to the end. Although this was undoubtedly true, the anecdote about his final words and being with Boxer to the end is used to reassure and manipulate the animals. Orwell suggests that leaders use emotive propaganda to control their people.

Squealer explains that the vet had bought the van from a knacker's yard and had not painted over the sign. Napoleon speaks in praise of Boxer at the next Sunday Meeting. He urges the animals to adopt Boxer's **maxims** of 'I will work harder.' and 'Napoleon is always right.' The pigs say they will hold a banquet in Boxer's honour and order a large crate of whisky from the money they've gained.

AQA exam-style question

How does Orwell portray ideas about class division in the novel *Animal Farm*?

Write about:

- how Orwell introduces ideas about class division throughout the narrative.

- how Orwell presents these ideas by the ways he writes.

[30 marks]

DO IT!

Why do you think the pigs tolerate Moses in this way?

DEFINE IT!

republic – an independent state recognised as a country

unanimously – without question or disagreement

STRETCH IT!

How does Orwell use Boxer's death to expose the reality of life on Animal Farm? Will any animal ever get to retire? How might this link to the return of Moses and his message about Sugarcandy Mountain?

Character and theme essentials

The end of Boxer

At the start of the novel, Orwell describes Boxer as looking 'somewhat stupid'. The end of Boxer is very upsetting but it was predictable. His removal and extermination shows the pigs' lack of care for other animals, no matter how loyal and hard-working they are. Boxer works himself to death for the greater good. He still believes that once the windmill is finished and he reaches his twelfth birthday, he will be allowed to retire. This blind optimism inevitability leads to disappointment. Although he is loved and cared for by the other animals (Clover and Benjamin), the removal and the sale of his body show that there will be no reward for hard work and loyalty on Animal Farm. The memorial banquet held in his honour is for the pigs alone who use the money made from selling his body to buy whisky. Boxer will be forgotten under the tyrannical rule of Napoleon and his descendants.

Benjamin

Both Benjamin and Clover show genuine concern and love for Boxer. This is juxtaposed with the pigs' indifference. It shows that even under tyrannical leadership, animals can still support one another. Clover and Benjamin both want Boxer to slow down. He has been badly injured in the Battle of the Windmill and yet stubbornly continues to work hard to complete the rebuilding of the windmill. Clover attempts to heal Boxer with sympathy and natural medicine. When Boxer collapses, Clover and Benjamin remain by his side.

Moses the raven returns

Moses the preacher returns to Animal Farm. He is both used and hated by the pigs. They allow him to stay and feed him beer. This shows that they know Moses is useful as he encourages the animals to believe their hard work on Earth will be rewarded after death when they will go to Sugarcandy Mountain. He is both a distraction from the difficulties of day-to-day life on Animal Farm and a motivator. The pigs keep him like a pet, just like Jones once did. This is another way in which the pigs have become like Jones.

Propaganda: rewriting history and reality; past and present

Squealer's job becomes challenging as he has to keep the animals motivated, further destroy Snowball's reputation, enhance Napoleon's reputation and cover up the sale of Boxer to the knacker. Squealer also uses the death of Boxer as an opportunity to praise Napoleon. He claimed to have been at Boxer's side when he died and reported that Boxer's final wishes were that the windmill be completed and that the animals remain loyal to Napoleon.

DOIT!

How does Squealer explain the words on the side of the van? What does this show about the continuing power of Propaganda?

Class division

Orwell clearly presents the widening of the class divide. During the harsh winter, all animals except the pigs and dogs have their rations reduced even further. The pigs are the elite and their dogs function as their army. Squealer argues that 'too rigid equality' is against the principles of Animalism. This makes no sense.

At the very top is Napoleon, who is elected President (unopposed) and drinks a full gallon of beer each day. In addition, Napoleon fathers thirty-one piglets. This new generation is educated by Napoleon himself.

DO IT!

1 List the negative aspects of the animals' lives under Jones and under Napoleon. Use these headings:

**Freedom   Work
Food   Comfort
Violence**

2 Under which ruler do the animals suffer the most?

REVIEW IT!

1 Which of Boxer's injuries is slow to heal?

2 When is Boxer due to retire and what will he receive?

3 Whose rations are reduced, again?

4 Who has almost been forgotten? What does this suggest about leaders?

5 How many piglets has Napoleon fathered?

6 Where and by whom are the piglets educated?

7 What do pigs wear on Sundays?

8 Why are the pigs growing so much barley?

9 Which extra ration do the pigs receive?

10 When does Animal Farm become a republic and who becomes President?

11 Who returns to preach? What does this suggest about life on the farm?

12 What happens to Boxer one summer evening?

13 What is coming out of Boxer's mouth?

14 Who keeps the flies off Boxer?

15 What does Squealer say Napoleon has arranged?

16 Where does Boxer stay for two days, and with whom?

17 Who reads the sign on the side of the van and what does it say?

18 What does Clover shout at Boxer?

19 Who claims to have heard Boxer's last words and what were they?

20 Squealer rewrites history several times. He persuades the animals that Boxer was taken to the vets. The animals believe him. Write a paragraph explaining your thoughts about this.

Chapter 10

Years pass

Summary

Years pass. Many animals die of old age and only Clover, Benjamin, Moses and the pigs can remember the time before the Rebellion. Clover is now 14 years old, two years past retirement age although no animal has ever retired. The farm is much more successful (financially) and the windmill is complete. It is used for milling corn rather than generating electricity. A new windmill is being built which will supposedly bring electricity to the farm but Snowball's dream of electrified stalls, hot water and the three-day week will never be realised as Napoleon deems this not to be in line with the spirit of Animalism. Instead, Napoleon preaches that hard work and basic living are the key to happiness. The pigs manage the farm. They do no physical work but produce an enormous amount of paperwork, which is then burnt. The animals still suffer (much as they did in Jones's day) from hunger, the cold, flies and the effects of hard work. However, Animal Farm is the only one in England run by animals and they all feel very proud about that.

The pigs parade

The end of Animal Farm shows us that life on the farm (for the majority of the animals) is the same as it was under Jones's rule. What were the animals promised that has not happened?

In the summer, Squealer leads the sheep away to a remote field where he teaches them a new song. Shortly after they return, Clover neighs in alarm when she sees Squealer walking on his hind legs. All of the pigs then come out of the farmhouse and parade around the yard on their hind legs. Napoleon appears carrying a whip. There is a moment when the animals may have protested but the sheep burst into their new song of 'Four legs good, two legs better!' while the pigs march back into the farmhouse. Clover leads Benjamin to the Seven Commandments wall and asks him if the words have changed. Only one commandment remains: 'All animals are equal but some animals are more equal than others.' In the days that follow, all the pigs supervising work carry whips. They buy themselves human gadgets, read human magazines and newspapers and wear human clothes.

Orwell presents the appearance of Napoleon and the other pigs walking on two legs as horrific. Look at Clover's reaction. Her neighing is high pitched and startled, showing her fear. Perhaps she has finally realised the pigs are essentially human in both their leadership style and their appearance. The timing is significant. The animals have just finished a day's work on a calm summer evening when Squealer makes his entrance into the yard. This juxtaposes the power of the pigs with the weakness of the workers.

The animals rush into the yard to see what Clover had seen.

> There was a deadly silence. Amazed, terrified, huddling together, the animals watched the long line of pigs march slowly round the yard. It was as though the world had turned upside-down.

This silence is effectively the death of hope and any illusion that all animals are equal: the revolution has failed; Animalism has ended.

Tour of inspection

Napoleon invites the neighbouring farmers to visit. The farmers play cards and drink. The animals creep up to the farmhouse to watch. Pilkington makes a speech in praise of Animal Farm. He equates the lower animals of Animal Farm with the lower classes.

Napoleon makes a speech of his own. He explains that the farm is a co-operative owned by the pigs. He announces that the animals will no longer be allowed to call each other comrade and that the custom of marching past a boar's skull every Sunday morning will cease. He points out that the farm's flag has had the hoof and horn removed from its design. Finally, he announces that the farm will revert to its original name of The Manor Farm. The animals outside creep away from the window and the pigs and farmers resume their card game.

From pig to man

As the animals walk away, they hear a violent uproar of voices from the farmhouse. They rush back to see what is going on. Napoleon and Pilkington have both played an ace of spades, meaning that one of them is cheating. The animals look in through the window and can no longer tell the difference between the pigs and the men. This is the climax of the novel. Why do you think Orwell chose to end on this image?

 STRETCH**IT!**

What has changed for the pigs? What have they gained as a consequence of the Rebellion? Was it inevitable that the pigs would become corrupted by power?

AQA exam-style question

How does Orwell portray ideas about hopes and dreams in the novel *Animal Farm*?

Write about:

- how Orwell introduces ideas about hopes and dreams throughout the narrative

- how Orwell presents these ideas by the ways he writes.

[30 marks]

Character and theme essentials

Napoleon

Napoleon not only walks on two legs; he transforms into a human. The whip represents his power and willingness to use violence as a method of control. He strolls around the garden, smokes a pipe and listens to the radio. He reads the newspaper and magazines. This implies he has leisure time while the animals work themselves into the ground. Orwell shows that leaders' lifestyles are funded by the working class. Napoleon now wears Jones's clothes, which include *leather* leggings. This use of another animal's skin as clothing is horrifying as it demonstrates his lack of respect for fellow animals. It is another demonstration of his power and superiority.

Pilkington

When the humans and pigs meet inside the farmhouse while the animals remain outside looking in, this shows the superiority of the pigs and foreshadows the inevitable end of Animalism. Pilkington (Napoleon's rival farmer) makes a toast that praises Napoleon for his achievements. He is impressed that Napoleon manages to get his animals to work so hard for such low rations and long hours. In effect, he praises his ability to exploit the working classes. He addresses the pigs and animals as gentlemen, which is hugely ironic as the pigs are neither gentle nor men. Napoleon responds, making it clear that the pigs are no different from the men and that his farm will be changed to remove several signifiers of Animalism (the flag, name, use of 'comrade'). Orwell's final ironic comparison is that either Napoleon or Pilkington is cheating at cards. We are left with the image of pig and man behaving so similarly that, like the animals, we can no longer tell the difference between the rule of men like Jones and Pilkington and the rule of Napoleon. Their voices and faces are indistinguishable.

Hopes and dreams

At the start of the chapter, Orwell insists, 'the animals never gave up hope'. They are proud of their farm and believe that, in time, Animalism will become fully realised. They nostalgically recount tales of the expulsion of Jones, the Seven Commandments and their achievements in the two battles. Old Major's vision would become a reality, one day. Even 'Beasts of England' was still secretly hummed.

The pigs, on the other hand, still aspire to greatness. Napoleon's dream of achieving a place among the 'great' men of England is realised and the pigs prosper at the expense of the other animals. It is clear that things have come full circle. The drunk masters of the farms argue and neglect the welfare of their animals. The cycle of corruption has become complete.

STRETCH IT!

Consider the way each leader compliments the other. What does this suggest about political leaders? How does Orwell show that relations between the pigs and farmers will not lead to lasting peace and cooperation?

REVIEW IT!

1. Which of the original animals are still alive?
2. What has happened to Napoleon and Squealer?
3. What has happened to the windmill?
4. Who has become richer?
5. What do the pigs do all day?
6. Animal Farm is unique in England. Why?
7. What are the sheep taught to chant? What is the effect of this chanting on the pig parade?
8. Why do the pigs have a parade?
9. Which pig leads the parade?
10. Which pig comes out last? What does he hold in his hand?
11. What has happened to the Seven Commandments?
12. What does Napoleon do in the garden?
13. What does Napoleon wear?
14. When the farmers come to visit, what do they do in the farmhouse?
15. Which farmer makes a speech praising Napoleon?
16. What changes to Animal Farm does Napoleon announce?
17. What do the animals notice about the faces of the pigs?
18. Why do Napoleon and Pilkington begin to argue?
19. When the animals look from pig to man, what is it impossible to say?
20. 'The novel ends where it begins, with drunk leaders neglecting their animals.' Write a paragraph explaining your thoughts about this statement.

Characters

Napoleon

What we know about Napoleon

- Napoleon is a large, boar who becomes the ruler of Animal Farm.

- He is Snowball's power-hungry rival.

- He uses violence and his army of dogs to control the other animals.

- He uses propaganda (Squealer) and changes the commandments to persuade and bully the animals into following his leadership.

- Napoleon is greedy. He sees financial potential in the windmill project. Orwell shows that there will always be those in positions of power who exploit the labour of others.

- Eventually, he becomes so similar to the human farmers it is impossible to tell them apart.

- Named after one of Europe's most famous revolutionaries, Napoleon turns a popular uprising into a dictatorship.

- If we take *Animal Farm* as an allegory of the Russian Revolution, Napoleon represents Stalin.

Napoleon helps to plan and deliver the Rebellion

In Chapter 2, Napoleon works with Snowball and Squealer to translate old Major's vision into Animalism. After the Battle of the Cowshed, Napoleon takes on the role of provider and hands out food to the animals. This makes him seem like a fair leader, but is he manipulating the animals?

Here are two students writing about Napoleon at the start of *Animal Farm*.

Student answer A

Orwell presents Napoleon as a strong but fair leader to begin with. He works well with Snowball and it is clear that he wants the farm to succeed. He is also considerate as he feeds the animals immediately after the battle 'double rations of corn to everybody'. Together, Snowball and Napoleon 'butted the door' of the farmhouse open, which shows they work together to lead the other animals. Napoleon is a confident leader who gives clear orders: 'Forward, comrades! The harvest is waiting', which shows he understands the importance of strong direction. This ensures the animals feel secure and guided in their actions.

Student answer B

Orwell foreshadows Napoleon's rise to power in several ways. Although he is shown working with Snowball, he is described as a 'fierce-looking boar' who is 'used to getting his own way'. This implies Napoleon is merely biding his time and using Snowball to establish a successful farm that he will then take over. What Napoleon doesn't do is significant. He does not get involved in educating the animals, destroying the whips or writing the commandments on the barn wall. This shows he does not believe in equality. His selfish nature is also shown when he takes the milk ('Never mind the milk, comrades!') which is later put into the pigs' mash. He also removes nine puppies that he educates privately. This is all part of his plan to seize control. He creates a personal army. Everything Napoleon does is driven by his lust for power.

Evidence

These students include two types of evidence to support their points: quotations within their sentences and reference to key events. It is vital to support your argument with lots of relevant evidence.

Napoleon becomes human

By the end, Napoleon and his pigs become just as bad as the human leaders. Initially, he uses Squealer to explain choices, but by the end does not even attempt to excuse his actions.

Napoleon versus Snowball

Orwell leads us to question whether we want leaders who charge with us into battle (Snowball) or leaders who give orders and observe as their people risk their lives (Napoleon). Napoleon's absence from the Battle of the Cowshed makes us question whether he is really a strong, brave leader. Snowball outshines him, and the animals admire Snowball's charisma and willingness to lay down his life for the cause. The windmill is initially Snowball's idea. Napoleon's disdain suggests that he rejects innovation (although he later suggests it was his idea) and refuses to collaborate with his opposition. This stubbornness and desire to dominate make Napoleon very unlikeable. Napoleon's focus on procuring arms (weapons) shows that he is happy to use violence as a means of protection and foreshadows his willingness to use violence to control his population. He trains his dog army for months, showing that he thinks long term about how to secure his position of power.

Orwell portrays Napoleon as violent to show us the horrific ways in which tyrants both secure and maintain their positions of power. When Napoleon realises the animals prefer Snowball as a leader, he uses his dog army to chase him off the farm. Snowball is then blamed for everything that goes wrong. Napoleon uses propaganda (Squealer) to rewrite the history of the Rebellion and casts Snowball in the role of traitor. Orwell wants us to question the 'histories' recorded by leaders. Are they always truthful accounts of the events?

 STRETCH IT!

What is Orwell suggesting about the nature of leadership in the way he presents Snowball and Napoleon?

Consider:

- their strengths and weaknesses as leaders
- their similarities and differences
- how Orwell wants the reader to respond to them.

Snowball

What we know about Snowball

- Snowball is another pig. To begin with, he works with Napoleon to lead the animals.

- Snowball represents the opposition to Napoleon's leadership.

- He is a creative, intelligent and inspirational leader who is very popular.

- The windmill is his idea.

- Snowball fights very bravely in the Battle of the Cowshed, charging straight at Jones and being shot. He is awarded a medal.

- He is passionate about education and wants all animals to understand Animalism.

- Snowball is chased off the farm by Napoleon's dog army.

- Once he has gone, Napoleon rewrites history to describe him as a traitor who acted as Jones's spy. He is accused of plotting against the animals, destroying the windmill and even being on Jones's side in the Battle of the Cowshed. Of course, he cannot defend himself.

- Orwell uses him to show the true spirit of revolution.

- If we take *Animal Farm* as an allegory of the Russian Revolution, Snowball represents Trotsky.

Snowball's intelligence

Orwell presents Snowball positively to encourage his readers to value intelligence. Snowball's desire to educate the animals and involve them in the decision-making process reflects the true spirit of Animalism, 'All animals are comrades'. Once Snowball was expelled from the farm, all education ceased. Due to their lack of education, the animals are badly equipped to challenge the authority of Napoleon or counteract Squealer's clever propaganda. Snowball also reads extensively and uses his new knowledge to plan the windmill. However, despite Snowball's intelligence, is he too trusting of Napoleon? He does not seem to question Napoleon's removal of the puppies, which become his dog army. Also, he accepts that the milk will be for the consumption of the pigs only. Snowball is therefore a flawed character but these minor flaws are nothing when you compare him with Napoleon's evil actions.

Snowball is described very positively by Orwell. However, once he has been expelled, Napoleon and Squealer use emotive language to destroy his reputation.

Orwell uses these words to describe Snowball:

vivacious inventive best at writing indefatigable hero often won passionate eloquence imagination

Squealer and Napoleon use these words to describe Snowball:

criminal the enemy traitor sheer malignity death sentence hiding mischief invisible influence menacing

Choose pairs of words (one from each list) and write paragraphs comparing Snowball's true character and the way he is presented within propaganda.

Read what one student has written about Snowball.

DO IT!

> Snowball was doomed from the start. He was full of optimism 'forward comrades' but was unlikely to ever achieve equality on the farm. This is because some animals were lazy, like Mollie. Although the working class, Boxer, were able to work very hard 'I will work harder' but were not intelligent enough to understand the great purpose of their cause. However, Orwell wants us to think Snowball would have been a better leader because of his genuine values and new ideas, 'more inventive'. He proved to be very intelligent as his plans for the windmill were very successful. In fact, some of the animals also learned to read such as Muriel and Benjamin but then either chose not to use these skills or had nothing to read. Snowball had great ideas but was never going to defeat Napoleon and create a world where 'all animals are equal'.

What are the strengths of this answer?

What can this student do to improve? For example: specificity, purpose and overall message.

Brave warrior

Snowball's second strength is his ability to plan defensive strategy and fight well in battle. Orwell is showing us the importance of strategy and defence in leadership. Without Snowball's planning, Animal Farm may well have been recaptured by the humans in Chapter 4. Snowball reads 'an old book of Julius Caesar's campaigns' to learn from other great leaders. This shows his dedication to protecting the farm and maintaining control. When he gives orders, every animal responds immediately. This united sense of purpose and belief shows Snowball is a great leader.

In the heat of the battle, Snowball proves his bravery by running straight for Jones who is armed with a shotgun. The unanimous decision to award Snowball 'Animal Hero, First Class' shows the universal love and respect Snowball inspires in the animals.

Old Major

What we know about old Major

- Old Major is the very well-respected boar who inspires the Rebellion. He is both impressive to look at and an impressive speaker.

- At his command, the animals gather in the barn and he inspires them with his vision of the future. He calls the animals comrades and teaches them 'Beasts of England'.

- He warns against becoming like man in terms of habits and behaviours (houses, clothes, alcohol, money, trade).

- Three nights after his speech, he dies in his sleep and is buried in the orchard. His spirit lives on; Clover recalls his vision after the purges.

- Orwell uses old Major to show the vision of revolutionaries and to explain the utopian vision of a society where all animals are equal.

- If we take *Animal Farm* as an allegory of the Russian Revolution, old Major represents both Karl Marx and Vladamir Lenin. Marx created Marxism, which underpinned communism in Russia. Lenin made the philosophy into a set of principles and led the Russian Revolution.

DO IT!

Re-read old Major's speech in Chapter 1. Write a list of the complaints he has about humans. How many of these describe Napoleon's actions?

STRETCH IT!

Old Major uses many persuasive techniques within his speech, such as rhetorical questions and emotive language. Make a list of his most powerful lines, identify his techniques and evaluate the success of his speech.

Squealer

What we know about Squealer

- He is a small, fat pig.

- He is an impressive talker who works for Napoleon to produce propaganda. Like Napoleon, he uses fear as a method of control.

- He has 'twinkling eyes' and swishes his tail when speaking to distract the animals from his lies.

Squealer has no problem with rewriting history and does whatever he can to maintain his privileged position close to Napoleon. At the start, when Snowball is still around, Squealer is insignificant. He is absent at the Battle of the Cowshed. However, after Snowball's expulsion, Squealer becomes an important player, explaining Napoleon's actions to the animals. He is often accompanied by the dog army, which makes him more persuasive.

Squealer trains the sheep to bleat propaganda slogans such as 'Four legs good, two legs better!'. He is the first pig to emerge from the barn on two legs in the final chapter. Squealer represents the power of propaganda within a political regime. Orwell wants us to question our own sources of 'news'. If we take *Animal Farm* as an allegory of the Russian Revolution, Squealer represents the vast media machine that presented the government's version of events in Russia. He represents Stalin's head of propaganda, Molotov.

Half-truths, omissions and plain lies

It is Squealer's job to ensure the animals only get Napoleon's version of the truth. This is to prevent them fully understanding the injustices of Animal Farm and to prevent any challenge to the leadership.

Complete the table. Which are half-truths, omissions or plain lies?

Issue	Squealer's response
Snowball's expulsion	• Napoleon had to expel Snowball to protect the other animals. • He was a criminal. • He came up with insane ideas, such as the windmill.
Napoleon's decision to build the windmill	• It was his idea all along. • He had pretended to oppose it to get rid of Snowball. It was tactical.
Napoleon's decision to trade with other farmers	• No commandment ever stated they should not trade. •
The pigs move into the farmhouse and sleep in beds.	• There was never a ruling against beds.
The windmill is destroyed.	• Snowball did it. •

Rewriting the Seven Commandments

One of Squealer's most important jobs is rewriting the Seven Commandments. In the final chapter, after the pigs parade on two legs, Benjamin and Clover see all the commandments have been removed except, 'All animals are equal but some are more equal than others.' This shows Squealer's ability to completely reduce and distort the principles of Animalism until they are completely contradictory to the teachings of old Major.

Do you agree with this student about the importance of Squealer? Why is propaganda so important?

Writing about Squealer

Read part of this student's essay about the importance of Squealer. Look at how they use evidence.

Without Squealer, who can 'turn black into white' using his skills of persuasion, Napoleon could not have remained in power. There are several points in the narrative where the animals look willing to unite against him. The most important person to persuade is Boxer. Squealer spends a lot of time explaining things to him using phrases such as 'Comrade Napoleon says' and 'You do not want to see Jones return'. When Squealer rewrites history to depict Snowball as a traitor at the Battle of the Cowshed, Boxer questions this and accuses him of lying 'I do not believe that'. Orwell shows that the population will sometimes question those in authority if they feel strongly about the issue. Boxer continues to protest until Squealer uses Napoleon's name. Boxer immediately changes his mind 'If Comrade Napoleon says it, it must be true'. This shows the danger of blindly believing in a leader. Orwell uses Squealer to show the value of propaganda within a dictatorship.

Boxer

What we know about Boxer

- Boxer is a very strong carthorse.

- Boxer is very close friends with Clover and Benjamin.

- Boxer fights very bravely in the Battle of the Cowshed. He is awarded a medal.

- Boxer wants to learn but is not very intelligent.

- He adopts personal mottos: 'I will work harder' and 'Napoleon is always right'.

- When the work or weather gets tough, he simply works harder.

- Napoleon attempts to set his dog army on him. Boxer easily defends himself.

- Boxer works himself to death. He is never allowed to retire and is sent to the knacker.

- Orwell uses him to show the plight of the ordinary worker within a dictatorship.

- If we take *Animal Farm* as an allegory of the Russian Revolution, Boxer represents the working-class majority.

Strong, brave and dedicated

Boxer's admirable attitude to hard work makes him valuable. Without Boxer, the farm would not survive. Orwell is suggesting that the most powerful and important part of a society is the working-class population. Boxer has the strength to overpower the pigs but chooses not to. He wants to be led and guided and is fully dedicated to the principles of Animalism. His strength is both physical and mental. These two aspects of strength mean Boxer is able to carry on when others struggle. We are supposed to care about and admire him. Orwell's sympathetic portrayal of the working class encourages us to align with them and see the pigs as an oppressive force. It is significant that only Boxer and Snowball receive medals for their bravery in the Battle of the Cowshed. His motto, 'I will work harder', gets him through, as well as the love and friendship he has for and receives from Clover and Benjamin.

From caring to killing

Boxer is a gentle giant. When he believes he has killed the stable boy in the Battle of the Cowshed, he is very upset. He says sorrowfully, 'I had no intention of doing that.' Later, when he is attacked by the dog army, Boxer could have killed the dogs easily but chooses not to. Finally, in the Battle of the Windmill, Boxer breaks the heads of three men. There is no evidence that he shows any remorse for his actions in the Battle of the Windmill. Perhaps Orwell is suggesting that Boxer's moral spirit has been eroded by relentless hard work and warns us of the dangers of complete obedience to ruthless leaders.

DOIT!

What do you think are the five most useful things to remember about Boxer? Use the bullet points below.

- Find five quotations.

- Summarise Boxer's symbolic significance.

- Link the way Boxer is treated to messages about equality.

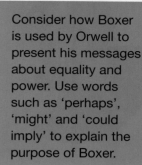

The exploitation of Boxer

Boxer's willingness to blindly obey leadership and work himself to death for the greater good makes him vulnerable to abuse and exploitation. Despite warnings from Clover and Benjamin, he continues to work extremely hard after the Battle of the Windmill.

Here are two students writing about Boxer's treatment.

Student answer A

Boxer's treatment during his illness and the disposal of his body are outrageous. He is ignored by the pigs and this shows Orwell believes the working class are exploited by leaders. Although Squealer appears 'full of sympathy' and gives Clover pink medicine, the pigs are more concerned with the running of the farm and make Clover and Benjamin work all day rather than letting them look after Boxer. I think it was a cruel plan to remove Boxer 'in the middle of the day' as the pigs wanted to sell Boxer to the knacker without the other animals knowing about it. Boxer's dreams of retirement and care in his old age were as fantastical as Moses' Sugarcandy Mountain.

Student answer B

Boxer's dream of 'peaceful days in green pasture' was never going to become a reality. His death and the sale of his body are symptomatic of the cruelty of Animal Farm. Boxer could not have worked harder or contributed more. Orwell's portrayal of the working class as dedicated and determined creates empathy for them and outrage at the way they are treated. It is clear that no animal will ever be respected or treated as equal. Clover works 'two years past the retirement age, and 'no animal ever retires'. The lives of the working class are portrayed as brutal, relentlessly challenging and provide no reward, except for the pigs. When Benjamin reads the words 'Horse Slaughterer' on the side of the van, the animals are rightly horrified. This should lead them to revolt against the pigs but, although they are all 'crying', they do not challenge Napoleon. The end of Boxer marks the end of Animalism and the end of hope. Orwell shows that in a dictatorship, the only winners are the elite. They have absolute control and will act ruthlessly to maintain it. The money made from selling Boxer is used to buy whisky, a recurring symbol of greed and corruption that contaminates those in power.

Jones

What we know about Jones

- Jones is a cruel drunk farmer and the original owner of Manor Farm. He is chased off it by the animals.

- He is a brutal farmer who uses whips, knives and chains on his animals and fires a gun which shows his brutal methods of control.

- Jones represents the greed of leaders who consume but do not contribute and is portrayed as a villain in old Major's speech.

- Ultimately, it is his failure to feed his animals that leads to them revolting.

- He is humiliated and spends hours in the local pub complaining.

- Jones tries to return but is defeated at the Battle of the Cowshed.

- Jones eventually dies in an old people's home but his spirit lives on as Napoleon becomes him.

- Orwell uses him to show why populations revolt against their leaders.

- If we take *Animal Farm* as an allegory of the Russian Revolution, Jones represents Tsar Nicholas II, the former leader of Russia.

STRETCHIT!

When writing about Napoleon's leadership, it is very useful to compare him to Jones. How are they similar and different? At what point do the animals realise what Napoleon has become? How would old Major have reacted to Napoleon's 'transformation'?

A cruel and evil leader

When the animals explore Jones's house, they are shocked and horrified by the luxuries he possessed. Of course, over time, the pigs will move into the farmhouse and become just as greedy. The house, which symbolises Jones's regime, is supposed to be locked up and made into a museum. Orwell is suggesting that new regimes often reject the trappings of the past but that this distinction is eroded over time. Perhaps all leaders are ultimately corrupted by greed and power.

The harness room also contains piles of tools that represent the cruel methods farmers like Jones use to control and kill their animals: bits, nose-rings, 'cruel knives…used to castrate' and so on. The burning of these items is celebrated by all animals and they believe that they will now live pain-free lives.

An ongoing threat used as a means of control

Jones becomes a threat used by Napoleon and Squealer ('Surely comrades, you do not want Jones back?') to silence the animals' protests. After a while, the animals cannot accurately remember what life was like under Jones. His name becomes synonymous with a living hell controlled by an evil tyrant. This becomes increasingly ironic as life under Napoleon's dictatorship becomes more and more unbearable.

 **DOIT!**

Look at the following luxury items found in Jones' home.

feather mattresses   **horsehair sofa**   **hams hanging**   **barrel of beer**

For each, explain why these items were so appalling to the animals. What do they represent?

Other characters

Frederick and Pilkington

Frederick is a cruel farmer who owns Pinchfield Farm. He is aggressive and violent towards his animals. Frederick succeeds in buying the timber from Napoleon but pays with fake banknotes. Frederick sends his men to attack Animal Farm in the Battle of the Windmill. He also blows up the windmill. After this, Frederick does not appear again. Orwell uses him to show the aggression of neighbouring leaders who want to take over the territory. If we take *Animal Farm* as an allegory of the Russian Revolution, Frederick represents Hitler, the ruler of Germany. Hitler and Stalin entered into an agreement but Hitler broke the pact.

Pilkington is a gentleman farmer who owns Foxwood. He manages his farm badly and spends all his time hunting and fishing. When Animal Farm is attacked by Frederick's men (Battle of the Windmill) and the windmill is blown up, he sends a note to Napoleon saying, 'Serves you right'. When playing cards at the end of the novel, both he and Napoleon play the ace of spades, which shows one or both of them has been cheating. They pretend to be friends but do not trust each other (rightly so!). Orwell uses Pilkington to show the hypocritical response of other countries to dictatorships. They will negotiate for financial gain despite their disapproval of the regime and its leader. If we take *Animal Farm* as an allegory of the Russian Revolution, Pilkington represents the UK. The final dinner party represents the Tehran Conference (1943) where the UK, USA and Russia met.

Make a list of similarities and differences between the three farmers: Jones, Pilkington and Frederick.

Clover

Clover is a middle-aged carthorse who is known for her kindness and maternal instincts. She is a close friend of Boxer. She is often disturbed by the injustices on the farm. She wants to learn and is a survivor. Orwell uses her to show the plight of the ordinary worker within a dictatorship. If we take Animal Farm as an allegory of the Russian Revolution, Clover represents the working-class majority. Clover and Boxer are always together. She continually warns him to stop working so hard but he ignores her. Despite this, she is loyal to him to the end. From her education of the next generation in Chapter 10 to her willingness to question the rewriting of the commandments, Clover demonstrates wisdom. She learns all the letters of the alphabet but is unable to blend them. This means she has to ask Muriel and Benjamin for help with reading. On several occasions, Clover's curiosity leads her to re-read the commandments. Although she accepts the changes, she is willing to question the pigs' intentions.

After the purges, Clover considers all that has happened and she cries for all they have lost. She compares old Major's vision with the reality of Napoleon, which shows her capacity to reflect and question those in authority. Although she feels powerless to defeat Napoleon, she still understands the injustices. Her decision to remain faithful and work hard is admirable, although Orwell shows passive resistance is ineffective.

DO IT!

What do you think are the five most useful things to remember about Clover? Use the bullet points below.

- Find five quotations.

- Summarise Clover's symbolic significance.

- Link the way Clover is treated to messages about equality.

Whymper

Whymper is the solicitor that helps Napoleon to trade with the humans. He is sly and sneaky and sees Animal Farm as a way of making money. Napoleon uses Whymper to spread positive propaganda. Orwell uses him to show the willingness of some outsiders to work with dictators for financial gain. If we take *Animal Farm* as an allegory of the Russian Revolution, Whymper represents all Westerners who catered to Russian interests and spread the mythical 'success story' of Stalinist Russia. One example is Lincoln Steffens, who said of Stalinist Russia, 'I've seen the future, and it works.'

The sheep

The sheep bleat whatever Napoleon and Squealer teach them. They are easily led and do not think for themselves. Orwell uses the sheep to show the danger of blindly following orders. If we take *Animal Farm* as an allegory of the Russian Revolution, the sheep represent those who believed Stalinist propaganda and spread the message without question.

Jessie, Bluebell, Pincher and the puppies

The dogs are Napoleon's army. They are dangerous and loyal and will carry out any of Napoleon's commands. The dog army is used to chase Snowball off the farm. Orwell uses the dogs to show how dictators create private armies to ensure they maintain power. If we take *Animal Farm* as an allegory of the Russian Revolution, the puppies represent the NKVD (Stalin's private and powerful secret police force).

Benjamin

Benjamin the donkey is the oldest animal and very cynical. He can read but mostly refuses to use this skill. Orwell uses Benjamin to show that, despite their intelligence, some members of society choose not to significantly contribute to society. Benjamin is unimpressed by Animalism and does not change his behaviour after the Rebellion. Orwell is showing that some recognise that any form of leadership will be corrupt and that there will be no difference between a world ruled by men and a world ruled by pigs. If we take *Animal Farm* as an allegory of the Russian Revolution, Benjamin represents cynical intellectuals who contribute little and achieve nothing.

Mollie

Mollie is a pretty but foolish white mare. Orwell uses her to show the unwillingness of some in society to give up luxuries for the greater good. If we take *Animal Farm* as an allegory of the Russian Revolution, Mollie represents the Russian Bourgeoisie/aristocracy who fled Russia when Stalin was in power.

Moses

Moses is Jones's pet raven. He does no work. Moses preaches about Sugarcandy Mountain (a heaven-like place). He is named after the prophet who received the Ten Commandments from God and led the enslaved Jews out of Egypt to safety. Orwell uses him to show the importance and power of hope and religion within a dictatorship. If we take *Animal Farm* as an allegory of the Russian Revolution, Moses represents the Russian Orthodox Church.

Minimus

Minimus is a pig poet used by Napoleon to write propaganda songs and poetry. Orwell uses him to show the power of propaganda. If we take *Animal Farm* as an allegory of the Russian Revolution, Minimus (along with the pigeons) represents *Pravda*, the Communist Party's newspaper.

The cat

The cat is a sly creature who does no work. Orwell uses the cat to show the role of the intelligence services within society. If we take *Animal Farm* as an allegory of the Russian Revolution, the cat represents the secret service agents who were replaced by Stalin's secret police (dog army).

 **REVIEW IT!**

1 Who gives a rousing speech about a world free from man? Find a quotation.

2 Who is the boar who gets his own way? Find a quotation.

3 Which boar draws up the plans for the windmill? Find a quotation.

4 Who is the very persuasive speaker who can 'turn black into white'?

5 Who are Boxer's two best friends?

6 How do they care for Boxer at the end of his life?

7 Which animal can read as well as the pigs but chooses not to use their talent?

8 Who loves ribbons and sugar and runs away?

9 Who preaches about Sugarcandy Mountain and what does he eat/drink?

10 Which animal joins a committee to talk to the birds?

11 Which farmer blows up the windmill?

12 Which farmer praises Napoleon at dinner?

13 Which farmer dies in an old people's home?

14 Who writes the new anthem, 'Animal Farm, Animal Farm'?

15 What are Frederick and Pilkington both worried about?

16 Who leads the animals in singing 'Beasts of England' after the purges?

17 How are the pigs and humans similar by the end of Animal Farm?

18 Who negotiates the deals between the pigs and humans?

19 Who privately educates the puppies? Why?

20 Who votes on both sides during old Major's meeting?

Themes and contexts

Power, leadership and corruption

In *Animal Farm*, Orwell exposes what happens when leaders become corrupted by power. Ultimately, corrupt leaders mean that all others within society suffer. Napoleon's corruption means that he thinks only of himself and members of his own species, and even then not all pigs are protected! Farmer Jones's power has corrupted him. Alcohol is a symbol of his corruption: he is cruel and selfish and neglects his animals.

Although it is easy to make links between the events of *Animal Farm* and the Russian Revolution (see pages 71–74), Orwell is really criticising corrupt leaders in general. You could swap Animalism for any other political ideology. It is not the political beliefs that underpin a society that are the problem: it is individuals who seize power and use it for their own selfish gain.

DOIT!

> **Snowball   Napoleon   Jones   Old Major   Frederick**
>
> For each leader, list five characteristics. Are any of them truly 'good' leaders? What makes a good leader?

Revolution and rebellion

DOIT!

> Write a list of reasons why the animals fail to create old Major's utopian society.
>
> - What could the animals have done differently?
> - Was Animal Farm doomed from the start?

Orwell is not criticising revolution or rebellion as actions to overthrow corrupt leadership. In fact, he praises the organisation, planning and execution of the original Rebellion at Animal Farm. The Rebellion is successful because of the vision of old Major, the planning and preparation by the pigs and the involvement of every animal collectively fighting for their freedom.

The Rebellion happens much more easily than the pigs expect. It is triggered by Jones's drunk behaviour and his neglect of the animals. When he forgets to feed and milk them, the animals break into the food store. When the men respond with whips, this triggers outrage and the Rebellion begins. The animals chase the humans off the farm. Orwell shows us that rebellions can catch leaders by surprise and can be triggered by very specific events.

STRETCHIT!

> Do you think Orwell teaches us that revolutions are pointless? If so, what else could be done to overthrow tyrants?

Revolution: coming full circle

By the end, Orwell has shown us that the Rebellion has simply resulted in one cruel tyrant replacing another. The parallels between Jones and the pigs are made explicit throughout. The final chapter concludes with the statement, 'The creatures outside looked from pig to man, and from man to pig, and from pig to man again; but already it was impossible to say which was which.' This shows that the animals feel hopeless. There is no way they can overthrow Napoleon. Or is there?

Rules, law and order

Orwell shows us that rules, laws and order are ways of controlling populations. Although initially the commandments are designed to benefit all animals, they are amended and rewritten to create double standards. Although pigs and other animals follow the same commandments, those in power can change the laws to suit themselves.

The Seven Commandments: inspiration

Orwell ironically presents the rules of Animal Farm as commandments. The Ten Commandments are a core part of Christianity and Judaism and have traditionally formed the basis for laws in England.

Make connections between some of the Ten Commandments and *Animal Farm*.

- You shall have no other gods but me.

- You shall remember and keep the Sabbath day holy.

- You must not commit murder.

- You must not steal.

1 How is Napoleon god-like?

2 What happens on Sundays after the Rebellion? How does this change?

3 Who commits murder? How and why?

4 Who steals? What do they steal and why?

Cruelty and violence

Although Animal Farm was supposed to be a peaceful place after the expulsion of Jones, violence is used to both intimidate and control the animals. Jones and his men used whips to brutally attack the animals and, by the end, Napoleon and his pigs appear carrying whips. The tools of violence represent the power the leaders have.

Jones: a cruel and violent farmer

Orwell portrays all violence as abhorrent. Sometimes Jones just neglects his animals but he also uses violence to control them. Old Major describes Man as a cruel creature who takes the animals' eggs, calves and foals.

Violence as part of revolution

Orwell accepted that reasonable force had to be used to overthrow dictators. The Rebellion itself occurs with a significant lack of bloodshed. Although the humans are kicked and butted, they all escape. This shows violence is only used by corrupt leaders. However, violence escalates at the Battle of the Cowshed where a sheep is killed and Snowball is shot.

STRETCH IT!

How does Orwell use sentence structure to explain the significance of the purges?

Napoleon's use of violence: the purges

Orwell shows Napoleon using violence to silence anyone who speaks out against him. Orwell is teaching us that leaders will use violence to control their populations. He uses his dog army to chase Snowball away and then to tear out the throats of 'rebel' pigs, chickens and others.

DO IT!

Look at this description of the results of the purges.

> And so the tale of confessions and executions went on, until there was a pile of corpses lying before Napoleon's feet and the air was heavy with the smell of blood, which had been unknown there since the expulsion of Jones.

1 How does Orwell show the horrific reality of Napoleon's decision to use violence?

2 How does he connect Napoleon and Jones? Why?

The hierarchy of society

- The Monarch: King or Queen
- Other royalty
- Aristocracy: lords, ladies, etc.
- Upper class: the very wealthy (land or money)
- Middle class: those in well-paid employment (doctors, lawyers, etc.)
- Lower/working class: those who often struggle to have enough money to live (food, shelter, clothing, etc.)
- Homeless, etc.

Class

The idea of social class is something that occurs within every society and every political system. Different systems divide the population into different groups, often according to wealth or family background. Historically, in the UK, people were divided into the social classes shown in the pyramid on the left.

Class division

Orwell believed in reducing class division. He wanted equal opportunities for all. He was disappointed by the results of the Russian Revolution as it failed to deliver true communism and equality.

Communism aims to remove the minority oppressive ruling class (bourgeoisie) to allow the majority working class (proletariat) greater freedom and equality. Communism aspires to provide the opportunity for all members of society to have equal voices, equal rights and equal access to resources.

Jones represents the bourgeoisie who keep the majority proletariat in a humiliating state of existence. The aim of the Rebellion is equality and, initially, this is partially achieved. The animals are united in their celebration; they move as one around the farm and sing 'Beasts of England' in unity. The whips and collars (symbols of slavery) are destroyed.

As Napoleon's power increases, equality decreases. By the end, the animals have returned to being enslaved. This is clear when the pigs appear on two legs, holding whips. They are now 'human' in both appearance and attitude. Napoleon is praised by Pilkington for his ability to control his 'lower animals' just as Pilkington has to manage his 'lower classes'. He is impressed that Napoleon's animals work so hard for so little food. The animals are enslaved because: 1 they are outwitted; 2 they are controlled by fear; 3 they agreed to follow the commandments (which have been changed); 4 they have blind faith in authority; 5 they have nowhere to go.

Religion

Orwell presents religion as a powerful force that can be harnessed by leaders and used to control populations. Moses the raven preaches regularly about Sugarcandy Mountain under Jones's leadership and then Napoleon's. Orwell portrays religion as a part of everyday life. Although almost all the animals unite behind Animalism (which you may say is their primary religion), their religious views are mostly kept private. Ultimately, Sugarcandy Mountain becomes an important thing to believe in when life on Earth is hard. The hope of a heavenly other world that the animals will go to after death is understandably important when their working life could be described as hellish.

Orwell describes Sugarcandy Mountain as situated 'somewhere up in the sky, a little beyond the clouds'. This makes the afterlife seem just out of reach. It is a promised place that can only be accessed after death. The enormous amount of food and rest available there shows what the animals desire in life. Sugarcandy Mountain (religion) is being used to blind the animals to their suffering. Karl Marx, a German philosopher whose writing would be well known to Orwell (see page 73), famously stated, 'Religion is the opium of the people'; similarly, Moses' tales of Sugarcandy Mountain serve as an opiate to numb the animals' feelings of misery.

Animalism: the new religion

If a religion is a system of belief, usually with a god-like central figure, it can be argued that Orwell depicts Animalism as a new religion. The commandments, church-like barn, singing of hymns ('Beasts of England'/'Animal Farm, Animal Farm'), prophets (old Major) and god-like authoritarian figure (Napoleon) all support this view. Napoleon is seen as god-like by the other animals. His word is 'gospel' and the masses (represented by Boxer) follow anything he says. Orwell wants us to consider the danger of blind devotion.

DO IT!

- Find five quotations that support the view that Napoleon is god-like.

- Is old Major also god-like? Why?

STRETCH IT!

Hymns begin as poems and are set to music. They are often full of persuasive or emotive language. Examine the lyrics of 'Beasts of England' and 'Animal Farm, Animal Farm'. How effective are these hymns as propaganda?

AQA exam-style question

How does Orwell use Moses and Napoleon to explore ideas about faith and religion in *Animal Farm*?

Write about:

- how Orwell presents the characters of Moses and Napoleon
- how Orwell uses the characters of Moses and Napoleon to present ideas about faith and religion.

[30 marks]

Consider the statement, 'Old Major's dream could never become a reality.' Write a list of arguments for and against this.

Hopes and dreams

Old Major's vision

Orwell uses old Major to present the dream of Animalism. He has a very clear vision of a flawless future where all animals are equal. This is a utopia that is unlikely to become reality. It is clear that the other animals are united in wanting a world free from the tyrannical rule of man. Of course, a dream will remain a dream unless a plan is put in place to make it a reality.

The death of the dream

Over time, old Major's vision is destroyed. The commandments are broken, rewritten and even 'All animals are equal' becomes 'All animals are equal but some are more equal than others.' Orwell shows that corrupt leaders abuse their positions of power: the dream becomes a nightmare. After the purges, the animals huddle on the knoll with Clover and she reflects on the differences between old Major's vision and the reality of life under Napoleon's tyrannical rule.

Old Major's vision	Life under Napoleon
• Animals are well fed.	• Animals are fed very little.
• Animals are no longer whipped.	• Animals are ripped apart by dogs and threatened with whips.
• The strong protect the weak.	• The weak are ignored or killed.
• All animals are equal.	• The pigs are the elite. Other animals are seen as inferior.
• 'Beasts of England' is sung by all as a symbol of unity.	• 'Beasts of England' is banned.

Hope

Even at the end, the animals believe there will be a time when animals will rule the Republic of England. It is very surprising that the animals remain hopeful. Orwell shows the animals' pride in the success of the Rebellion: the farm is run *by* animals *for* animals. Old Major's vision remains. Their memories of 'old heroic days' when humans were defeated are powerful enough to keep hope alive.

The Russian Revolution

George Orwell believed in equality and socialism. Socialism is the belief that all people should be treated as equals and that the country's resources should be shared fairly. Socialists believe that the rich should support the poor but do not demand the absolute equality that communism does. In the UK, socialist governments introduced ideas such as the National Health Service (NHS), free education and council housing. This support network was called the 'Welfare State'. Orwell believed that communism was unachievable but that socialism would solve much of the world's inequality caused by capitalists (see page 73).

Joseph Stalin

Animal Farm can be seen as a direct criticism of Stalinist Russia. Orwell saw Stalin's 'Purges' first-hand. He was fighting in the Spanish Civil War against the dictator Franco, when on Stalin's orders, Spanish fighters carried out a purge of their own: Orwell saw many of his friends being killed.

Who's who in the Russian Revolution

Character in *Animal Farm*	Description	Who they represent in the novel
Napoleon	Large boar	Stalin (dictator of the USSR; under Stalin, the Soviet Union was transformed from a peasant society to an industrial and military superpower; he ruled his people through terror.
Snowball	Intelligent boar	Trotsky (Russian revolutionary)
Squealer	Small fat pig	Molotov (Stalin's head of propaganda)
Boxer	Male carthorse	The working-class majority
Clover	Female carthorse	The working-class majority
Benjamin	Old donkey	Cynical intellectuals
Mollie	White mare	Russian bourgeoisie/aristocracy
Moses	Raven	Russian Orthodox Church
The cat		Former secret service agents
Jones	Human farmer	Tsar Nicholas II
Whymper	Human lawyer	Westerners who spread the mythical successes of Stalinist Russia
Frederick	Human farmer	Hitler/Germany
Pilkington	Human farmer	UK
Old Major	Old boar	Lenin (Russian revolutionary) and Marx (German philosopher who developed the theory of international communism)
Minimus	Pig	*Pravda*, the Communist Party's newspaper
The dogs		NKVD (Stalin's private and powerful secret police force)
The sheep		Uninformed masses

Stalin and the Russian Revolution

An allegory

Animal Farm is an allegory, which means, in this case, that the characters and plot represent real people and events. The real events Orwell is referencing took place in Russia between 1917 and 1943. Orwell makes the events much simpler to show the corruption and horror more clearly.

Tsar Nicholas II

Nicholas II had ruled Russia since 1894. He and the rest of the upper class (including the Russian Royal Family) owned the majority of Russia's land, property and wealth. There was huge inequality and he was hated by the majority of working-class Russians.

Two revolutions; two battles

Leon Trotsky

The Russian Revolution was actually two revolutions (the October and February Revolutions). Orwell presents these as the two battles (Cowshed and Windmill). The February Revolution was an uprising caused by the working-class people suffering and starving. The second October Revolution led to a new Communist government taking over Russia. The old leader, Tsar Nicholas II, left Russia. Later, the whole Russian Royal Family was murdered. Within the new leadership, there was a power struggle between Stalin and Trotsky (Napoleon and Snowball). Trotsky believed in world revolution whereas Stalin wanted Russia to be strong and independent.

How Russia was changed

The old Russian Empire had been populated by farmers and peasants. It focused on agriculture and small farms run by individuals and families. However, under the new leadership, Russia became industrialised and farms were joined together. This joining of farms was called collectivisation. Anyone who objected to this new system was murdered. Orwell shows this when the hens rebel against giving up their eggs: they are killed by the dog army. In the early days, free speech was valued but was later banned. Russia became totalitarian.

Adolf Hitler

Stalin and Hitler

Shortly before the Second World War (late 1930s), Stalin tried to take advantage of the conflict between Germany and West Europe. This ended in disaster when Hitler invaded Russia in 1941, despite Hitler and Stalin signing an agreement to work together in 1939. This is shown where Frederick and Napoleon strike a deal over timber that ends in disaster.

Communism

Russia became a Communist country. Communism is where everything is owned by everyone. In theory, there should be total equality. All people should own all property and share all resources equally. This is what Karl Marx wanted to achieve. Orwell believed the Russian Revolution did not achieve the aims of communism.

Communism: EQUALITY	Socialism: SOCIAL SUPPORT	Capitalism: INDIVIDUALISTIC, COMPETITIVE and MONEY-DRIVEN
• All people are equal. • Resources should be shared equally. • Property is not owned but shared. • All wealth is publicly shared. • There is no class system. • Everyone works together. There are no business owners.	• All people are equal. • Resources should be shared fairly. • Some property is privately owned but some is publicly shared. • Some wealth is privately held but some is publicly shared. • There is reduced class division. • Workers have rights and are treated with respect by business owners.	• Inequality improves competition. • Resources will not be shared equally. • Property is privately owned. • Wealth is held by individuals. • There is more class division. • Workers are paid wages by business owners.

DO IT!

Re-read the 'Who's who' on page 71. Answer the following questions.

1 How are Jones and Nicholas II similar? Find quotations to support your view.

2 How are Animalism and communism similar? Find quotations to support your view.

The reality of communism: farming

In Russia, the principle of communism became diluted and Stalin created forced labour camps and introduced collectivisation. The small farmers were forced to give their land to Stalin to create huge farms. They were then made to work on these state farms. If you refused (and thousands did), you were killed. The collectivisation programme resulted in severe disruptions to food production and led to mass starvation. Millions died. Between 1928 and 1934, Russia lost 70–90 per cent of sheep, cows and horses. These horrific facts were hidden as Stalin used propaganda to tell his people that there were no problems with food production. Stalin spread his messages of 'success' to capitalist countries such as the UK. Consider what Whymper is led to believe about Napoleon's resources.

The reality of communism: the Great Purge

Stalin systematically murdered Russians who disagreed or protested. They were tortured and publicly put on trial before being executed. Stalin set up a department that organised the trials and executions. The work of this group was called the 'purges'. What was supposedly a workers' paradise became a brutal dictatorship.

Orwell's messages

Inspiration

Orwell was inspired to write *Animal Farm* when he saw a boy riding and whipping a carthorse. He considered how easily the horse could destroy the boy if it knew its own strength. This reminded him of the strength of the workers and the cruelty of the leaders within dictatorships.

What was Orwell against?

1 Dictators

2 Inequality

3 Hypocritical leaders

What did Orwell want?

1 To show how power corrupts individuals

2 To expose the inequality within society

3 To show how leaders exploit their populations

4 To reveal the brutality of life under Stalin

5 To show that revolutions can be successful

Different interpretations

Orwell himself said that although he wanted to expose the 'myth' of Russian communist success, he was writing more generally about the dangers of revolutions that result in one master being replaced by another. Immediately after the Rebellion, Napoleon and the other pigs take the milk for themselves. This is the point at which Orwell believed the other animals should have confronted their leaders. If the animals had worked together to ensure the leadership was free from corruption, Animal Farm could have become more like old Major's vision.

STRETCH IT!

Independently research how readers' attitudes to *Animal Farm* might have changed over time. Make a poster or leaflet that explores these changes.

Consider:

- attitudes to *Animal Farm* in 1945 in the UK (when Stalin was a British and American ally in the Second World War)

- attitudes to *Animal Farm* in 1945 among the Russian working class

- attitudes to *Animal Farm* in 1945 of Stalin and his government

- attitudes to *Animal Farm* in 1953, after Stalin's death, when it was widely known he had murdered millions of Russians during the purges

- attitudes to *Animal Farm* today, from a modern perspective since the end of Communist Russia

- your own attitude to *Animal Farm*.

REVIEW IT!

1 What are the names of the six leaders in *Animal Farm*?

2 Why is Jones an appalling leader?

3 What is a philosophy? Give an example from *Animal Farm*.

4 The Rebellion comes full circle. Why?

5 Which two major world religions have commandments at their core?

6 Old Major warns the animals against becoming like the human farmers. What is banned?

7 How is Jones presented as violent?

8 Napoleon uses the purges to silence those who speak out against him. What happens to the air after the purges?

9 What are the bourgeoisie and the proletariat?

10 What does communism aim to do, regarding the bourgeoisie?

11 Why is Sugarcandy Mountain important for the animals?

12 How is Animalism similar to a religion?

13 At the end of the novel, what hope remains?

14 What two core beliefs did Orwell have?

15 What is *Animal Farm* an allegory of?

16 What was collectivisation?

17 What happened to the cows, sheep and horses as a result of collectivisation?

18 Which Russians did Stalin systematically murder during the purges?

19 What was Orwell against? (Name three things.)

20 What did Orwell want? (Name five things.)

Language, structure and form

Language

Orwell makes choices in the language he uses to convey his meanings. This includes words (vocabulary), phrases and techniques. When we analyse language, we are identifying Orwell's methods and considering their impact.

Descriptions of the animals

Orwell creates clear visual impressions of his characters by using **adjectives** to describe their appearance. However, it is through the ways in which the animals move and speak (as well as what they say and don't say) that Orwell often presents their true nature and symbolic significance.

The voices of the animals

Each significant animal is given a distinctive voice. Squealer always uses rhetorical questions and direct address: 'Surely, comrades, you do not want Jones back?' Boxer uses repetition: 'I will work harder.' Clover uses gentle persuasion and says cautiously: 'I am *almost* certain I saw this.' Orwell does this to show what type of character they are: for example, Squealer is manipulative, Boxer is blindly devoted and Clover is kind and timid.

Let us examine Orwell's presentation of old Major.

Appearance

> 'Twelve years old', 'grown rather stout', a 'majestic-looking pig'

Orwell presents old Major as old and therefore wise.

Orwell portrays old Major as weighty and therefore important.

By presenting old Major as a pig of prestige, Orwell presents him as important, superior in intellect and powerful. The proper noun 'Major' also implies this and is similar phonetically to 'Majesty'.

How does he move?

> 'On a sort of raised platform, Major was already ensconced on his bed of straw'

Old Major is positioned above the others. This implies he is respected and god-like.

Old Major is settled in a comfortable position. This implies he is an experienced speaker and secure in his position of authority.

Old Major rests comfortably on straw, which implies he is happy being an animal, like the others. The noun 'bed' implies he is resting and foreshadows his imminent death.

How does he speak?

Orwell wants old Major's message to be clearly understood. He projects it across the barn for all to hear. Orwell is signifying the importance of this vision.

'He cleared his throat and began'

The verb 'began' implies old Major will tell the animals a story. Orwell suggests that narratives within visions are essential to win over the hearts and minds of the majority.

What does he say?

Orwell's inclusion of the collective noun 'comrades' introduces the allegorical aspect of the narrative. Comrades are persons of equal significance involved collectively in a form of resistance or revolution. This emotive term is used within old Major's speech to unite the animals.

Orwell uses the adverb 'Now' to imply urgency within old Major's message. Orwell implies old Major will take time to present his ideas but he hopes for imminent change.

'Now, comrades, what is the nature of this life of ours?'

This philosophical rhetorical question is used by old Major (Orwell) to encourage both the animals and readers to consider their greater purpose. The inclusive pronoun 'our' unites the audience and asks them to imagine a future for the benefit of all.

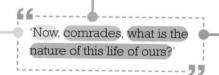

Orwell's use of speech

Orwell uses direct speech for most of the animals. This is when we read the words as spoken. To begin with, this is true for Napoleon too. His first words are, 'Never mind the milk, comrades!', which shows he is confident ordering the other animals around and clearly selfish, as the milk is taken from them. However, after Snowball is expelled, Napoleon's speech is always written as reported speech. We never hear directly from him. This makes Napoleon seem remote and god-like. During the debate about the windmill, both Snowball's and Napoleon's speeches are reported. Perhaps Orwell is saying that all leaders are untrustworthy.

Orwell's use of irony

Orwell uses irony to point out the problems on the farm. If something is ironic, it means it is the opposite of what would be expected, for example, if all animals are equal, the milk should be shared equally but the pigs keep it for themselves. This is irony. In old Major's speech, every criticism he makes of humans can be applied to Napoleon. This is an example of **situational irony** as Napoleon is supposed to support Animalism and work to prevent such injustices (for example, no animal is supposed to live in the farmhouse but the pigs move in and Napoleon has his own room). Orwell uses situational irony to show the inequality of Animal Farm. Orwell also uses **verbal irony** frequently in Squealer's and Napoleon's speeches (for example, when Napoleon commands that there should be a 'Spontaneous Demonstration'. A planned demonstration cannot, by definition, be spontaneous!). Verbal irony is used by Orwell to show the hypocrisy and unfairness of life on Animal Farm.

DO IT!

Look at the first appearance of each of the main characters (mostly Chapter 1) and the first time they speak. For each, record quotations about their appearance, movements and how they speak (as well as what they say). What is the significance of these different descriptions?

Narrative voice

Orwell uses an external **narrator** or storyteller. This use of a third person (the narrator knows everything and shares this with us) allows us to listen to a traditional storyteller explaining the events. It is a simple but effective way of showing the horrific events that occur on Animal Farm.

Third person but with a key difference

A third person narrator can tell us everything. However, at key moments, Orwell chooses to tell us about important events from the perspective of one of the animals. For example, after the purges, Clover is crying. She recalls old Major's vision and compares it with the brutal reality of life under Napoleon's leadership. However, she will 'remain faithful, work hard…accept the leadership'. These moments are included to make us question why the animals do not rebel against such injustice. By showing their stupidity, Orwell warns us to think critically about society and leadership.

Time

Time passing is shown in a simple way. **Phrases** such as 'All through that Summer' and 'Three nights later' allow us to understand the consequences of four years of events. It is chronological (the events occur in the right order), which again makes the story simple and clear. Memories are used at key moments but are always linked to present events. Old Major remembers his childhood and Clover remembers old Major's vision after the purges.

Propaganda

Orwell tells his story using a clear and straightforward style. This allows us to see clearly how leaders such as Napoleon and Squealer use language in a manipulative way. Orwell is showing us how powerful propaganda is. The animals not only believe what they are told but change their behaviours and attitudes as a result. When Jones is in charge, they are so outraged by the inequality on Manor Farm they revolt. Yet, by the end, they have been brainwashed so successfully by Napoleon and Squealer they accept his leadership without question.

Propaganda to unite

To begin with, Orwell shows the pigs using slogans and songs to unite the animals. Even old Major does this with 'Beasts of England'. The Seven Commandments are taught to the animals and the single maxim 'Four legs good, two legs bad!' is used to ensure all animals believe in the core principles of Animalism. This shows the power of propaganda to unite populations.

Four legs good, two legs bad!

Humour

Although the events within *Animal Farm* are deeply disturbing, Orwell encourages us to laugh at the foolishness of the animals in order to learn from their mistakes.

Mocking religion

The **hyperbolic** description of the blissful nature of Sugarcandy Mountain suggests such places do not exist. Here, Orwell criticises both those who preach about and those who believe in such places. Through the obvious links between the place of plentiful food and the animals' starvation, Orwell shows how religion offers hope and reassurance to the animals that their hard work will be rewarded. They may suffer now but it will all be worth it in the end!

> Orwell's use of the adjective 'mysterious' implies that Sugarcandy Mountain is otherworldly.

> Orwell's use of inclusive **alliteration** 'all animals' implies that Moses presents religion to appeal to every creature as all will finally be equal in the afterlife.

> He claimed to know of the existence of a mysterious country called Sugarcandy Mountain, to which all animals went when they died. It was situated somewhere up in the sky, a little distance beyond the clouds, Moses said.

> Orwell's use of **sibilance** implies that Moses is not speaking the truth but simply deceiving the animals (like Satan in serpentine form in the Garden of Eden).

> Orwell satirises religious preachers who promise heaven-like places that are just out of, but soon to be within, reach. The phrase 'little distance' implies that the animals will be rewarded before long if they are faithful and push through the challenging times ahead, **metaphorically** represented by the clouds.

Mocking propaganda: poetry and songs

The poetry of the poet pig Minimus is truly awful. The poem 'Comrade Napoleon' is full of clichés. Lines such as 'Lord of the swill-bucket' are funny but also show why Napoleon is powerful.

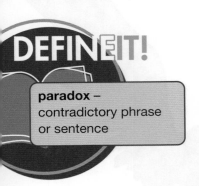

DEFINE IT!

paradox – contradictory phrase or sentence

Symbols and names

Orwell uses often-recurring symbols and names to 'signpost' his messages.

The farm (and its name)

The farm itself is a microcosm for the whole of society. It has borders, limits on who is allowed in and out and is ruled by a leader.

At the start: Jones calls it 'Manor Farm'. The farm sounds grand and wealthy, even though Jones is neither. A manor is a large house in which wealthy people (often members of the aristocracy) live. Their servants live nearby (in a separate, less luxurious part of the building or in basic accommodation nearby). This class division is shown by the contrast between the luxury of the farmhouse and the cold, harsh places the animals have to sleep. The farmhouse is feared by the animals as it represents cruel leadership.

After the Rebellion: the new name, 'Animal Farm', represents equality. The farmhouse is going to be turned into a museum.

By the end: the pigs live in the house. When Napoleon changes the name back to 'Manor Farm', it is clear that old class divisions have been re-established.

Seven Commandments on the barn wall

At the start/after the Rebellion: the Seven Commandments represent law and order. The erosion and rewriting of these shows how Animalism is destroyed by Napoleon's greed and corruption.

By the end: only one commandment remains: 'All animals are equal but some are more equal than others.' This paradox shows that Animalism has been destroyed.

THE SEVEN COMMANDMENTS

1. Whatever goes upon two legs is an enemy.
2. Whatever goes upon four legs, or has wings, is a freind.
3. No animal shall wear clothes.
4. No animal shall sleep in a bed.
5. No animal shall drink alcohol.
6. No animal shall kill any other animal.
7. All animals are equal.

Structure

Chronological

Orwell uses this logical and straightforward way of organising events to clearly show the erosion of Animalism. Each event destroys another part of old Major's vision: as the pigs' power increases, the animals' power decreases; as the pigs become more human and masterly, the animals are treated more like animals and slaves. This represents the class system being restored.

Cyclical

Orwell uses a **cyclical structure** to show that the pigs have become as bad as the humans. Orwell begins with a vision of drunk humans who neglect their animals. It ends with this too. Orwell shows the Revolution has simply led to one corrupt, greedy leader being replaced by another.

Repetition

Orwell uses the repetition of key maxims such as 'Four legs, good two legs bad!' to show the power of propaganda and slogans. When these are altered ('Four legs good, two legs *better*!') Orwell's use of repetition ensures we notice the changes made to this maxim and the commandments. Boxer's foolish repetition of 'I will work harder' shows his blind devotion to the cause. Orwell criticises both those who create and those who repeat such simplistic slogans. He encourages us to think beyond these catchphrases. Orwell also repeats 'comrade' throughout (79 times). The word loses all meaning as class division increases and the leaders and animals are far from equal.

Foreshadowing

Orwell gives us lots of dark hints about the later events in *Animal Farm*. Old Major's speech is full of warnings about the future. These include Boxer being sent to the knacker, the animals being forced to work until death and the chickens having their eggs stolen from them. This is ironically foreshadowing life under Napoleon.

The use of the dog army is foreshadowed when Napoleon takes the puppies away for private education. Orwell wants us to question the actions of those in power. What are their motives?

The stealing of the milk foreshadows the inequality that grows between the pigs and the other animals. Orwell shows us how even minor inequalities lead to greater inequality later.

DOIT!

Re-read old Major's speech. How many of his predictions come true? What is Orwell suggesting about leaders?

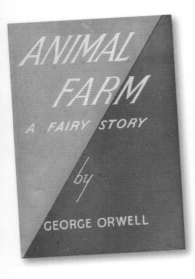

Form

Orwell subtitled *Animal Farm* 'A Fairy Story'. This has two meanings:

1   a children's story about magical creatures and other worlds

2   a story that is untrue.

Perhaps Orwell is suggesting that true equality is impossible: a fantasy. Or perhaps he wants us to learn a lesson from the mistakes the animals make. Fairy stories often end happily with good defeating evil, dreams coming true and all problems being overcome. From this, children learn to behave and conform in order to gain reward. The distressing ending of *Animal Farm* is created by Orwell to educate us about the realities of revolution and corrupt leaders. The ending is happy – for the pigs! The dream of Animalism is destroyed and all that is left is for the animals to suffer until death.

An animal fable

Animal Farm is also an animal fable. A fable is a short story involving animals that teaches a moral lesson. It is an ancient form of storytelling and is used across the world to educate both old and young. The animals are personified and we are able to learn lessons about humanity through examining their choices and the consequences. Orwell chooses specific animal species to reflect aspects of humanity (the greedy pigs, the obedient sheep).

Political satire

Satire is a type of comedy used to criticise a part of society. The criticism is obvious enough to be understood by the majority of readers, but hidden beneath a ridiculous situation to allow us to laugh at the problems of society. Orwell ridicules power-hungry dictators by setting his satire on a farm and portraying the cruel leader as a greedy pig.

An allegory

An allegory is a story that hides its true meaning beneath a very different plot. There is a moral message and each character represents a part of humanity or society. *Animal Farm* is usually described as an allegory because of the multiple clear links to real people and events; Napoleon/Stalin, Snowball/Trotsky and so on. Allegories often use very simple language and put across clear moral messages.

Some critics have said that *Animal Farm* is simple enough to be a 'children's story'. Write a list of arguments for and against this statement.

STRETCHIT!

How is storytelling used within Orwell's narrative?

Consider:

- who tells stories

- who listens and believes

- why the stories are told

- the impact of the stories.

1 What makes *Animal Farm* a fairy story?

2 How does Orwell ridicule power-hungry dictators?

3 What is the farm a microcosm of?

4 How does Orwell's style of writing in *Animal Farm* help us to understand his message?

5 Give an example of foreshadowing in the novel. What is its effect on the reader?

6 Why does Orwell use dramatic irony?

7 Why does Orwell use verbal irony to describe the 'Spontaneous Demonstration'?

8 What four aspects of description does Orwell use to portray his characters?

9 What is the difference between direct and reported speech?

10 Does Orwell use a first, second or third person narrator?

11 At key moments, Orwell's use of third person shifts. How?

12 How does Orwell present the power of propaganda such as slogans and songs?

13 Why does Orwell include humour?

14 What does Mollie trying on ribbons represent?

15 Why is Sugarcandy Mountain described hyperbolically?

16 In what way is 'Comrade Napoleon' different to 'Beasts of England'?

17 Why is the second line from the song 'Animal Farm, Animal Farm' ironic?

18 Why does Orwell use **chronological** structure?

19 Why does Orwell use a cyclical structure?

20 How does old Major's speech foreshadow later events?

Doing well in your AQA exam

Understanding the question

Carefully preparing to answer the exam question is vital. If you are not clear in your mind about what the question is asking for, then there is a real risk that your answer will include irrelevant ideas and evidence.

Below is an AQA exam-style question. The question itself has been prepared by a student so that they fully understand it. Look at their notes.

NAILIT!

Read the question carefully and understand it. Make sure you focus on answering the question. Don't just write whatever you know about the novel. Your answer must be relevant to the question.

What methods and **techniques** does Orwell use?

Napoleon is a character created by Orwell. What is his role? What does he symbolise?

Make sure the focus is on Napoleon, and compare/contrast everything with him.

AQA exam-style question

How does Orwell use the **character** of Napoleon to explore ideas about **leadership** in *Animal Farm*?

Write about:

- what Napoleon says and does and what happens to him
- how Orwell presents Napoleon and other leaders.

What does Orwell have to say about this? What different models of leadership does he give us?

Might we react in ways that Orwell could not predict?

This student has studied the question carefully and realised that:

- the focus is on Napoleon and leadership generally
- 'how' means you need to focus on methods (language, form and structure) and their effects
- leadership needs to include links to **context** (for example, the Russian Revolution, leaders, tyrants, general ideas about leaders)
- what we think and feel about Napoleon has been shaped and controlled by Orwell.

'Pinning the question down' in this way has allowed the student to make sure that they have really thought about what the question is asking. In the examination room it is very easy to misread questions, answering the question that you want or expect to see, rather than the question that is actually there. The method outlined here will support you as you begin to find some useful ideas to support your answer.

Choose another question from earlier in this guide. 'Pin the question down' as above.

Planning your answer

You have 45 minutes for your response; 5–10 minutes spent preparing the question and planning your answer is time well used. It will help make sure your answer is clear and relevant. Practise preparing and planning.

Once you have pinned down your question properly, planning an answer will be quite straightforward. Your brief plan should set out:

- your key, *relevant* ideas
- the content of each of four or five paragraphs
- the order of the paragraphs.

Here is the same student's plan for the question on page 84. They have allowed 10 minutes for planning and 35 minutes for writing.

NAILIT!

High-level answers should have an overarching **argument** that is developed through the essay.

Paragraph	Content	Timing plan
1	Brief introduction. Use the words of the question and 'pinning the question down' to establish the focus of the answer and develop a line of argument.	9.15am
2	Napoleon and Snowball. Two styles of leadership. Compare their belief and methods. Link to Russian Revolution. Trotsky and Stalin.	9.17am
3	Old Major's vision and Napoleon's reality. Orwell's criticism of leaders who distort visions of equality for personal gain. Lenin/Marx. Marxism and Stalinist Russia.	9.24am
4	Napoleon and propaganda. Orwell uses Napoleon and Squealer to expose the dangers of propaganda as a method of control. Stalin and Molotov.	9.31am
5	Napoleon's use of violence. The purges. Russian Revolution and Stalin.	9.38am
6	Brief conclusion. Refer back to question. My view today/1945 audience. Check answer.	9.45am

Sticking to the plan

Note how this student has jotted down time points for when they should move on to the next section of their answer. That way, they make sure they do not get stuck on one point and fail to cover the question focus in enough breadth.

Planning to meet the mark scheme

The plan above suggests that the student has thought carefully about the task in the question, that they are familiar with the mark scheme for their AQA Modern text question and are planning to cover its requirements. (See the summary mark scheme on page 86.)

DOIT!

Go back to the exam question that you chose for the Do it on page 84. Develop a brief plan for it as above.

Assessment objective	What the plan promises
AO1 (Response to task and text)	Understanding Orwell's messages about leadership. Focus on Napoleon as a construct. Wide ranging overview of Napoleon's actions and use of propaganda (what he says and does).
AO2 (Identification of writer's methods)	Analysis of propaganda techniques, foreshadowing, cyclical structure, irony and symbolism.
AO3 (Understanding of ideas/perspectives/context)	Russian Revolution, Stalin, Molotov, purges, general ideas about leadership, view of Napoleon and corruption today and in 1945.

What your AQA examiner is looking for

Your answer will be marked according to a mark scheme based on four assessment objectives (AOs). The AOs focus on specific knowledge, understanding and skills. AO4 – which is about vocabulary, sentence structures, spelling and punctuation – is worth just four marks. Together, the other AOs are worth 30 marks, so it is important to understand what the examiner is looking out for.

Mark scheme

Your AQA examiner will mark your answers in 'bands'. These bands loosely equate as follows:

- band 6 approx. grades 8 and 9
- band 5 approx. grades 6 and 7
- band 4 approx. grades 5 and 6
- band 3 approx. grades 3 and 4
- band 2 approx. grades 1 and 2.

Most importantly, the improvement descriptors in the table below will help you understand how to improve your answers and, therefore, gain more marks.

The maximum number of marks for each AO is shown.

Assessment objective (AO)		Improvement descriptors				
		Band 2 Your answer…	Band 3 Your answer…	Band 4 Your answer…	Band 5 Your answer…	Band 6 Your answer…
AO1 12 marks	Read, understand and respond	is relevant and backs up ideas with references to the novel.	often explains the novel in relation to the question.	clearly explains the novel in relation to the question.	thoughtfully explains the novel in relation to the question.	critically explores the novel in relation to the question.
	Use evidence	makes some comments about these references.	refers to details in the novel to back up points.	carefully chooses close references to the novel to back up points.	thoughtfully builds appropriate references into points.	chooses precise details from the novel to clinch points.
AO2 12 marks	Language, form and structure	mentions some of Orwell's methods.	comments on some of Orwell's methods, and their effects.	clearly explains Orwell's key methods, and their effects.	thoughtfully explores Orwell's methods, and their effects.	analyses Orwell's methods, and how these influence the reader.
	Subject terminology	sometimes refers to subject terminology.	uses some relevant terminology.	helpfully uses varied, relevant terminology.	makes thoughtful use of relevant terminology.	chooses subject terminology to make points precise and convincing.
AO3 6 marks	Contexts	makes some simple inferences about contexts.	infers Orwell's point of view and the significance of contexts.	shows a clear appreciation of Orwell's point of view and the significance of contexts.	explores Orwell's point of view and the significance of relevant contexts.	makes perceptive and revealing links between the novel and relevant contexts.

AO1 Read, understand and respond/Use evidence

Make sure you read and answer the question carefully. The examiner will be looking for evidence that you have answered the question given. Do not make the mistake of going into the exam with an answer in mind. Knowing the novel well will give you the confidence to show your understanding of the novel and its ideas as you answer the question on the paper in front of you.

Using evidence means supporting your ideas with references to the novel. They can be indirect references – brief mentions of an event or what a character says or does – or direct references – quotations. Choose and use evidence carefully so that it really does support a point you are making. Quotations should be as short as possible, and the very best ones are often neatly built into your writing.

AO2 Language, form and structure/Subject terminology

Remember that *Animal Farm* is not real life. It is a novel that Orwell has *created* to entertain and influence the reader. The language and other methods he uses have been chosen carefully for effect. Good answers will not just point out good words Orwell has used: they will explore the effects of those word choices on the reader. You must refer to the writer, showing that you understand that the novel is a construct at all times, to progress beyond Grade 3.

Subject terminology is about choosing your words carefully, using the right words and avoiding vague expressions. It is also about using terminology *helpfully*. For example, here are two different uses of subject terminology, the first much more useful than the second:

> ### Student answer A
>
> Orwell foreshadows Napoleon's brutality in Chapter 2: 'a large, rather fierce-looking boar.' The listing of 'large, rather fierce' implies he has both the physical strength and angry attitude to get what he wants

> ### Student answer B
>
> Orwell uses a list: 'large, rather fierce'.

AO3 Contexts

Context is important when it helps the reader to understand the meaning and ideas within the novel.

- How might readers in the UK in 1945 have responded to this criticism of the Russian Revolution and Stalin's leadership?

- How might your view of leadership and propaganda be affected by Orwell's ideas?

- How might we reconsider equality in our democracy today?

The best answers will include contextual information that is directly relevant to the *question*, not just the novel in general. See pages 66–75 for more information and guidance on how to make the most of contexts in your writing.

AO4: Vocabulary, sentence structures, spelling and punctuation

Make sure that you use a range of vocabulary and sentence structures for clarity, purpose and effect. Accurate spelling and punctuation is important too for this assessment objective.

NAILIT!

To boost your marks when answering questions do the following:

- Know the novel well. Read it and study it.

- Don't go into your exam with ready-prepared answers.

- Read the question and make sure you answer it thoughtfully.

- Choose details in the novel that will support your points.

- Don't treat the novel and its characters as though they are real. Instead ask why Orwell has chosen to create those words, or that event. What effect is he trying to achieve?

Writing your answer

Getting started

You have looked at one student's plan, and you will have noticed that they have decided to write a short introduction. Here are the openings of two students' answers to the question on page 84 about how Orwell uses Napoleon to explore ideas about leadership in *Animal Farm*.

> **Student answer A**
>
> Napoleon is portrayed as a thoroughly despicable character. His leadership style is abhorrent and his willingness to use violence as a method of control is terrifying. Orwell has carefully constructed this appalling tyrant to expose the horrific reality of life under dictators such as Stalin. However, it is the weakness of the other animals and their willingness to follow such leadership that is really shocking.

> **Student answer B**
>
> I am going to explain why Napoleon is a bad leader. Orwell made him evil like Stalin to show Stalin was a bad leader and teach the audience not to support men like Stalin. He has animals killed and threatens them a lot too. These are the points I'm going to tell you about in my essay.

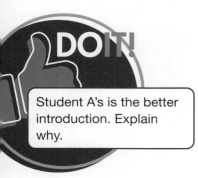

DOIT!

Student A's is the better introduction. Explain why.

The response

Look at the student's plan for their essay on page 85. Here is part of the second paragraph of their answer. Note the way they use very brief quotations to help them comment on Orwell's methods and their effects. An examiner has made some comments in the margin.

Orwell portrays two very different leadership styles in Napoleon and Snowball. He does this to emphasise the different ways in which leaders can act. For example, Snowball is heroic in the Battle of the Cowshed where he joins the others and exclaims, 'Forward, Comrades!' Although using an imperative to direct the animals, he participates in the battle too and is shot by Jones. He is the embodiment of equality and is willing to sacrifice his own life for the greater good of Animalism. Orwell portrays this form of leadership as heroic and admirable. In contrast, Napoleon is nowhere to be seen, which implies he either plays no part in the Battle or performs badly. Napoleon's earlier use of the collective noun 'Comrades' is attached to an imperative, 'Never mind the milk.' However, he uses imperatives to shut down debate rather than inspire. The order is given and Napoleon selfishly seizes the milk to give to the pigs. Orwell's use of these imperatives shows that although both leaders give orders and portray themselves as the animals' equals (comrades), one is doing it for selfish reasons and the other selfless. Orwell forces us to question the intention and meaning of political rhetoric.

Direct evidence well used; embedded within the argument.

Effect of the words is clearly explained

Precise terminology

The effects are explored in detail.

Links to Orwell's intentions

Paragraph topics

The rest of your paragraphs should each deal with a subtopic of the main focus of the question. Here, the question focuses on Napoleon and leadership. The student's plan suggests that the next three paragraph topics will be: old Major's vision and Napoleon's reality, Napoleon and propaganda, and Napoleon's use of violence.

Below, you can see how – in their 'Napoleon and propaganda' paragraph – the same student makes detailed references to the key words in the question so as to stay sharply relevant. The references are underlined to point them out.

> Napoleon's leadership would have failed without propaganda. He uses many methods to control what the animals think, feel and how they behave. Orwell is exposing the power of propaganda within society. It is a vital tool for leaders. By teaching his animals the Seven Commandments and 'Four legs good, two legs bad!', Napoleon ensures all animals feel like they are working together for the greater good. This strong leadership unites the population. However, when Napoleon uses Squealer to change the commandments, this exposes him as a liar. Orwell is criticising leaders who are not open and honest with the people and encourages us to question our leaders' motives.

Using evidence:

This student uses indirect evidence by referring to the kind of words used when they are uncertain of the whole quotation and uses direct evidence in the form of quotations when they know them. Both forms of evidence are valid.

Ending your answer

If you write a conclusion, make it useful: don't simply repeat what you have already said. The answer we have been looking at ends with this summary:

> Overall, I believe that Orwell's portrayal of Napoleon as a sadistic, evil dictator is an effective way to critique both Stalin's leadership of Russia and other dictators. However, Orwell also uses Napoleon to expose the hypocrisy and methods of control used by the majority of leaders throughout history. The use of propaganda and fear as methods of control are evident across the world today. Orwell's portrayal of Napoleon makes us question our leaders, their motivations and their methods.

DO IT!

Use the preparation and planning you did for your chosen exam question (see Do it! on page 84) to write a full answer.

STRETCH IT!

Develop a range of evaluative vocabulary to enable you to pinpoint Orwell's intention. Use words like:

- condemns
- criticises
- exposes
- ridicules
- subverts
- questions

Going for the top grades

Of course you will always try to write the best answer possible, but if you are aiming for the top grades then it is vital to be clear about what examiners will be looking out for. The best answers will tend to:

• show a clear understanding of both the novel and the exam question • show insight into the novel and the question focus • explore the novel in relation to the focus of the question • choose evidence precisely and wisely	AO1
• analyse Orwell's methods and their effect • use relevant, helpful subject terminology	AO2
• explore aspects of context that are relevant to the novel and question.	AO3

A great answer **will not** waste words or use evidence for its own sake.

A great answer **will** show that you are engaging directly and thoughtfully with the novel, not just scribbling down everything you have been told about it.

The best answers will be RIPE with ideas and engagement:

R	• Relevant	Stay strictly relevant to the question.
I	• Insightful	Develop relevant insights into the novel, its characters and themes.
P	• Precise	Choose and use evidence precisely so that it strengthens your points.
E	• Exploratory	Explore relevant aspects of the novel, looking at it from more than one angle.

Find an essay or practice answer you have written about *Animal Farm*.

Use the advice and examples on this page to help you decide how your writing could be improved.

Below is part of a student's answer to: How does Orwell use the character of Napoleon to explore ideas about leadership in *Animal Farm*?

Next to the answer are some comments by an examiner.

It is clear that throughout this allegorical novel Orwell uses simplistic characterisation to bluntly convey his opinions of Stalin and other dictators. His own experiences fighting on the communist side in the Spanish Civil War clearly show his political bias. With this in mind, Napoleon was always going to represent the most horrific aspects of the far right. This 'fierce-looking Berkshire boar' is ambitious and brutal. The emotive adjective 'fierce' implies that he will use violence when he becomes leader and the plosive alliterative 'Berkshire boar' signifies his forceful nature. The choice of animal is significant as old Major was also a boar, which implies that his class status will assist him in becoming the leader of Animal Farm. Orwell's portrayal of Napoleon as a boar 'with a reputation for getting his own way' effectively foreshadows his inability to share and therefore support Animalism in theory or practice. It is an all too tragic reality that characters with such qualities are able to become leaders of companies, territories and even nations.

Precise terminology covering language, form and structure

Confident point about purpose links to Orwell's intentions

Specific and original link to context

Direct evidence well used. Embedded within the argument.

Effect of the words is detailed and perceptive

REVIEW IT!

1 In your exam, how long should you spend preparing, planning and writing your *Animal Farm* answer?

2 Other than *Animal Farm*, what texts will you need to write about in Paper 2 (Modern texts)?

3 How many *Animal Farm* questions will be on the paper?

4 How many questions should you answer on *Animal Farm*?

5 Here is a template for an essay question for *Animal Farm*. Create your own exam questions by filling in the brackets.
How and why does [name of character] change in *Animal Farm*? Write about:
- how [name of character] responds to other characters
- how George Orwell presents [name of character] by the way he writes.

6 Here is a template for an essay question for *Animal Farm*. Create your own exam questions by filling in the brackets.
How does George Orwell explore [theme] in *Animal Farm*? Write about:
- the ideas about [name of theme] in *Animal Farm*
- how George Orwell presents these ideas in the way he writes.

7 Here is a template for an essay question for *Animal Farm*. Create your own exam questions by filling in the brackets.
Do you think [name of character] is an important character in *Animal Farm*? Write about:
- how George Orwell presents [name of character]
- how George Orwell uses [name of character] to present ideas about [theme].

8 How long should you spend planning and preparing your answer?

9 Why is it important to prepare or 'pin down' your exam question?

10 What is meant by an indirect reference to the novel?

11 Why is it helpful to check your vocabulary, sentence structures, spelling and punctuation during your exam?

12 How many marks are AO1, 2 and 3 worth together?

13 What does AO1 test? How many marks are allocated out of 30?

14 What does AO2 test? How many marks are allocated out of 30?

15 Your friend has told you that they are going to learn an essay that they wrote in the mock exams as their revision. What would you say to them?

16 'Introductions and conclusions are not essential.' Is this true or false?

17 In the month leading up to your exam, what is a useful strategy to help you with your revision?

18 Plan a five-paragraph answer to the question you created in question 5 above. (Or you could use this question: Do you think Squealer is an important character in *Animal Farm*? Write about:
- how George Orwell presents Squealer
- how George Orwell uses Squealer to present ideas about people and society.)

19 Plan a five-paragraph answer to the question you created for question 6 in this Review it quiz (or you could use this question: How does Orwell explore power and corruption in *Animal Farm*? Write about:
- ideas about power and corruption in *Animal Farm*
- how George Orwell presents power and corruption by the way he writes.)

20 Use the plan you made in question 18 or 19 above to write an answer in no more than 40 minutes.

NAILIT!

In the month leading up to your exam, all your revision should be based on planning and writing answers to exam questions. You will find plenty of exam questions in this guide for practice.

AQA exam-style questions

NAILIT!

Make sure that you only choose **one** question in the examination. Your examiner will only give you marks for one response.

On these pages you will find six practice questions for *Animal Farm*. In your exam you will have a choice of two questions. You only need to answer one. The question is worth 30 marks plus four marks for spelling, punctuation and grammar (total marks 34).

PRACTICE QUESTION 1

How does Orwell use events in *Animal Farm* to explore ideas about the consequences of rebellion?

Write about:

- some of the events in the novel
- how Orwell uses these events to explore ideas about the consequences of rebellion.

[30 marks]
AO4 [4 marks]

PRACTICE QUESTION 2

How does Orwell use Boxer and Benjamin to explore attitudes to revolution in *Animal Farm*?

Write about:

- what Boxer and Benjamin say and do
- how Orwell uses Boxer and Benjamin to explore attitudes to revolution.

[30 marks]
AO4 [4 marks]

PRACTICE QUESTION 3

How does Orwell explore the use of propaganda by leaders?

Write about:

- types of propaganda and their purpose.
- how Orwell uses examples of propaganda to explore ideas about leadership.

[30 marks]
AO4 [4 marks]

PRACTICE QUESTION 4

How does Orwell present the consequences of old Major's vision in *Animal Farm*?

Write about:

- the consequences of old Major's vision
- how Orwell presents the consequences of old Major's vision

[30 marks]
AO4 [4 marks]

PRACTICE QUESTION 5

How does Orwell present the importance of birds on the farm?

Write about:

- the ways in which birds affect what happens on the farm
- how Orwell presents the importance of the birds.

[30 marks]
AO4 [4 marks]

PRACTICE QUESTION 6

In *Animal Farm*, Boxer says 'Napoleon is always right'. How does Orwell explore attitudes towards leaders in the novel?

Write about:

- how Orwell presents some of the attitudes towards leaders
- how Orwell uses these attitudes to explore ideas about society.

[30 marks]
AO4 [4 marks]

Glossary

adjective A word that describes a noun (for example: *tame* raven; *enormous* beast).

allegory A fictional story that has a moral message.

alliteration Words starting with the same sound and placed near each other for **effect** (for example: the animals are called to the 'big barn' to emphasise its significance).

character A person/animal with human attributes in a novel created by the writer (for example: Napoleon, Mr Jones, Moses).

characteristic The words or actions a writer gives a **character**.

context The circumstances in which a novel is written or is read. For *Animal Farm*, these could include normal beliefs in 1945 about government or propaganda.

cyclical structure A storyline that ends at the same place or point that it begins. See **structure**.

dialogue The words that **characters** say in novels.

dramatic irony This is when the reader knows something the characters do not. See **irony**, **situational irony** and **verbal irony**.

effect The impact that a writer's or **character's** words have on the reader; the mood, feeling or reaction the words create in the reader.

foreshadow A clue or a warning about a future event.

hyperbole (hyperbolic) Over the top, exaggerated language (for example: wretched).

imagery The 'pictures' a writer puts into the reader's mind. **Similes** and **metaphors** are particular forms of imagery. We also talk about violent, graphic or religious imagery, and so on.

imperatives Instructions or commands.

irony (ironic) 1 Mild sarcasm. A technique sometimes used by writers to mock a **character** and make them appear ridiculous or dishonest. 2 An event or result that seems to be the opposite of what could reasonably be expected. This causes a sort of bitter amusement to the victim (for example: it is ironic in *Animal Farm* that the pigs end up drinking alcohol – one of the principles of Animalism is that 'No animal shall drink alcohol.').

juxtapose (juxtaposition) Place or deal with two things close together for contrasting effect (for example: in Chapter 3, Boxer's physical strength is contrasted with the pigs' intelligence).

linear structure The order in which events are presented corresponds to the order in which they happen. See **structure**.

maxim A short, pithy statement expressing a general truth or rule of conduct.

metaphor (metaphorically) Comparing two things by referring to them as though they are the same thing. (For example: when Moses talks of Sugar Candy Mountain, the clouds could be seen as a metaphor for the struggles the animals need to go through in order to reach the afterlife.)

microcosm A small world represented a much larger one.

narrator A storyteller. In *Animal Farm*, Orwell uses third person omniscient (a method of storytelling in which the narrator knows the thoughts and feelings of all of the characters).

pathetic fallacy Where nature is used to reflect human emotion (for example: the gentle pastoral scene in Chapter 2 is used to imply that good has conquered evil).

personification A **metaphor** when a person is used as a symbol for a particular idea or characteristic (for example: Jones as the personification of tyranny).

phrase A group of words within a sentence.

rhetoric The art of effective or persuasive speaking or writing, especially using techniques such as **hyperbole**.

rhetorical device Persuasive language technique.

rhetorical question A question asked in order to create a dramatic effect or make a point rather than to get an answer.

rhyme A close similarity or connection of the sound between words or the end of words.

rhythm The 'beat' in prose, poetry or music.

satire (satirise) The use of humour to criticise those in authority or society more generally (often political).

sibilance A figure of speech in which a hissing sound is created within a group of words through the repetition of the 's' sound.

simile Describing something by comparing it with something else (for example: All that year the animals worked like slaves').

situational irony When the outcome of an event is the opposite of the likely outcome. See **dramatic irony**, **irony** and **verbal irony**.

structure (structurally) The way in which the events in a novel are ordered (for example: *Animal Farm* is arranged in ten chapters and uses a **cyclical structure**).

subject terminology The technical or special terms used in a particular subject.

symbol(ise) A symbol is something that represents something else. Using symbols can be a way for the author to influence a reader without them realising.

technique Another word for method. Writers use different techniques to create different **effects**.

verbal irony When someone says the opposite of what they mean. See **dramatic irony**, **irony** and **situational irony**.

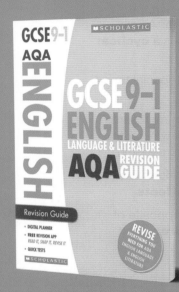